INCREDIBLE ENGLISH
Class Book 4

1	Playing outdoors	3
2	Art	11
3	Health	19
4	On the farm	27
5	Animal life	35
6	Safety	43
7	At school	51
8	Underwater life	59
9	Technology	67
	Festivals	75
	Children around the world	78
	Syllabus	84
	Wordlist	86

Peter Redpath
Michaela Morgan   Sarah Phillips

1 Playing outdoors

1 Look, listen and repeat. 1.1   **2** Listen and find. 1.2

1 swim   2 climb   3 row   4 skateboard   5 fish   6 waterski   7 sail   8 rollerblade
9 play football   10 play basketball   11 play tennis   12 play hide and seek

3 Ask and answer.

Can you waterski?   Yes, I can.

Can you play tennis?   No, I can't.

Outdoor activities

Unit 1 3

5 Read and find the picture.

- a Archie's got a football.
- b Jazmin's got a basketball.
- c Luke, Finn and Archie are playing football.
- d Eve's got rollerblades.
- e It's five o'clock in the morning.
- f Eve's reading a book.
- g Coco's resting next to Eve.
- h Jazmin's got tennis balls.

6 Which sentence is in the story? Make more sentences. PMB page 6

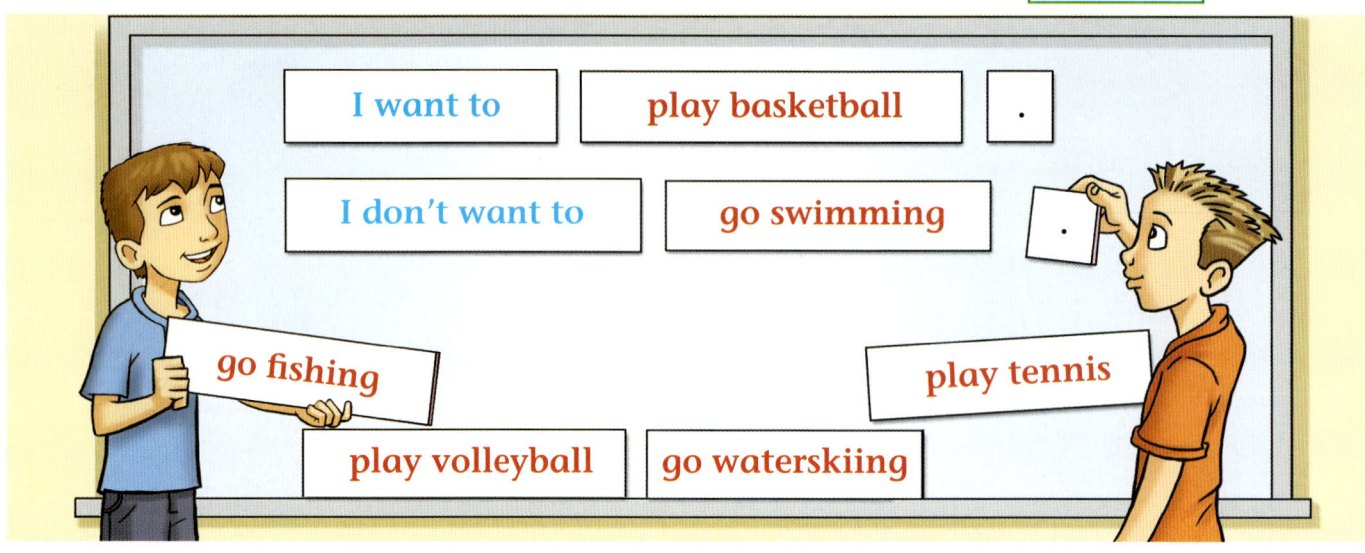

7 Listen and say which picture. 1.5

8 Play the game.

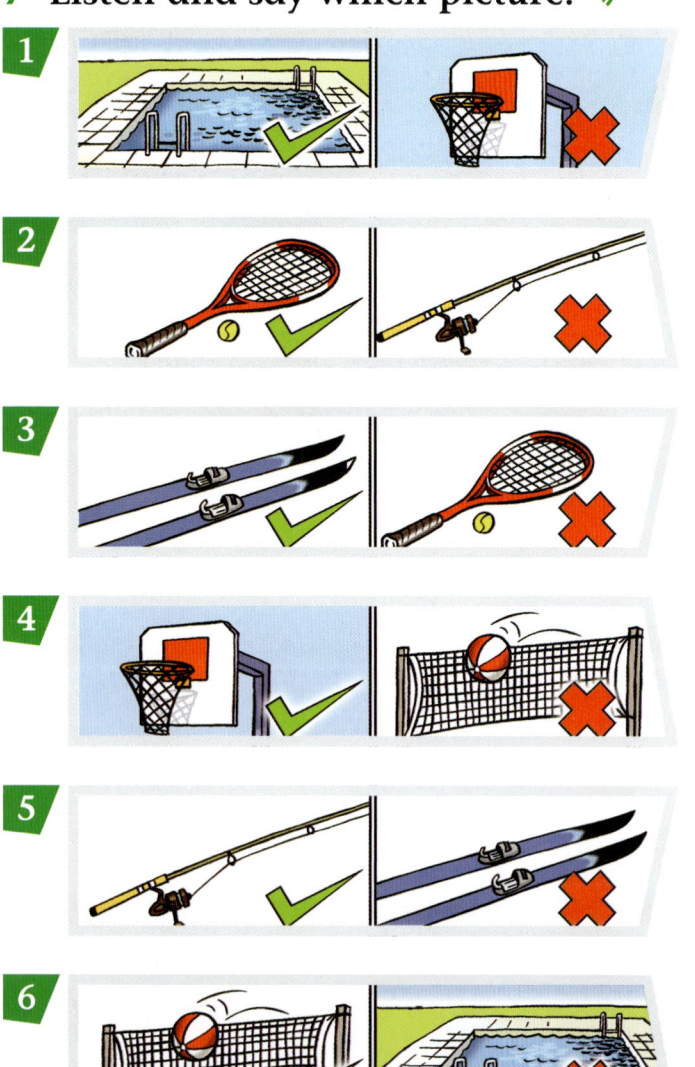

I want to go swimming.
I don't want to play basketball.

Picture 1?

Yes!

Unit 1

I want / don't want to go swimming.

Emails

9 Read and answer the questions.

A

To: finchfamily@mymail.co.uk

Subject: Hello!

Dear Mum and Dad,

I'm having a fantastic time at the Incredible Adventure Camp. There are lots of things to do. Every day I go fishing with Archie and I play tennis with Eve. Molly and Jazmin go sailing every morning.

Love,
Luke

B

To: jimandbetty@onemail.co.uk

Subject: Having fun!

Dear Mum and Dad,

It's great here! The countryside is beautiful. You can do so many sports! You can go rowing and sailing, and you can play basketball or volleyball every day.

I love the camp but I'm very tired – the children always want to get up very early but I want to stay in bed!

I hope you're both well.

Love,
Eve xx

1. Who likes the countryside?
2. Who goes fishing with Archie?
3. Who goes sailing every morning?
4. Who plays tennis with Eve?
5. Who wants to stay in bed in the morning?

10 Listen and read. Then sing the song. 1.7

song

Let's go swimming,
Come and swim with me!
Let's go swimming,
Come and swim with me!
I like swimming – do you like swimming too?
Let's go swimming, I want to swim with you.

Let's go fishing,
Come and fish with me …

Emails • Playing together

Unit 1 7

The water cycle and the weather

Learn about the water cycle and talk about the weather

11 Look, and read.

12 Listen, read and find. 🔊 1.8

Rain comes from the water in the sea. First, the sun shines on the sea. It warms the water. **Can you find this?**

The water becomes water vapour. This process is called evaporation. The wind carries the water vapour up into the sky. **Can you find this?**

High in the sky the air is cooler. When the water vapour meets the cooler air, it becomes very small drops of water that form clouds. This process is called condensation. **Can you find this?**

The small drops of water join together and become rain drops. The raindrops are bigger and heavier than the clouds and fall to the ground. It's raining!

Can you find this? If it's very cold or high in the mountains, it snows. **Find this.** The rain falls into the rivers and the rivers carry the water back to the sea. And it starts all over again! This is the water cycle.

13 Read and choose.

1 It shines on the sea.   water vapour / the sun
2 It becomes clouds.   the sun / water vapour
3 It becomes rain.   small water drops / cool air
4 The air is cooler here.   high in the sky / near the sun
5 It carries the water to the sea.   a cloud / a river

14 Look, listen and repeat. 🔊 1.9　　**15** Listen and find. 🔊 1.10

a It's sunny.
b It's cloudy.
c It's windy.
d It's raining.
e It's snowing.
f It's foggy.
g It's stormy.
h It's 10 degrees.
i It's minus 5.

Talk about it!

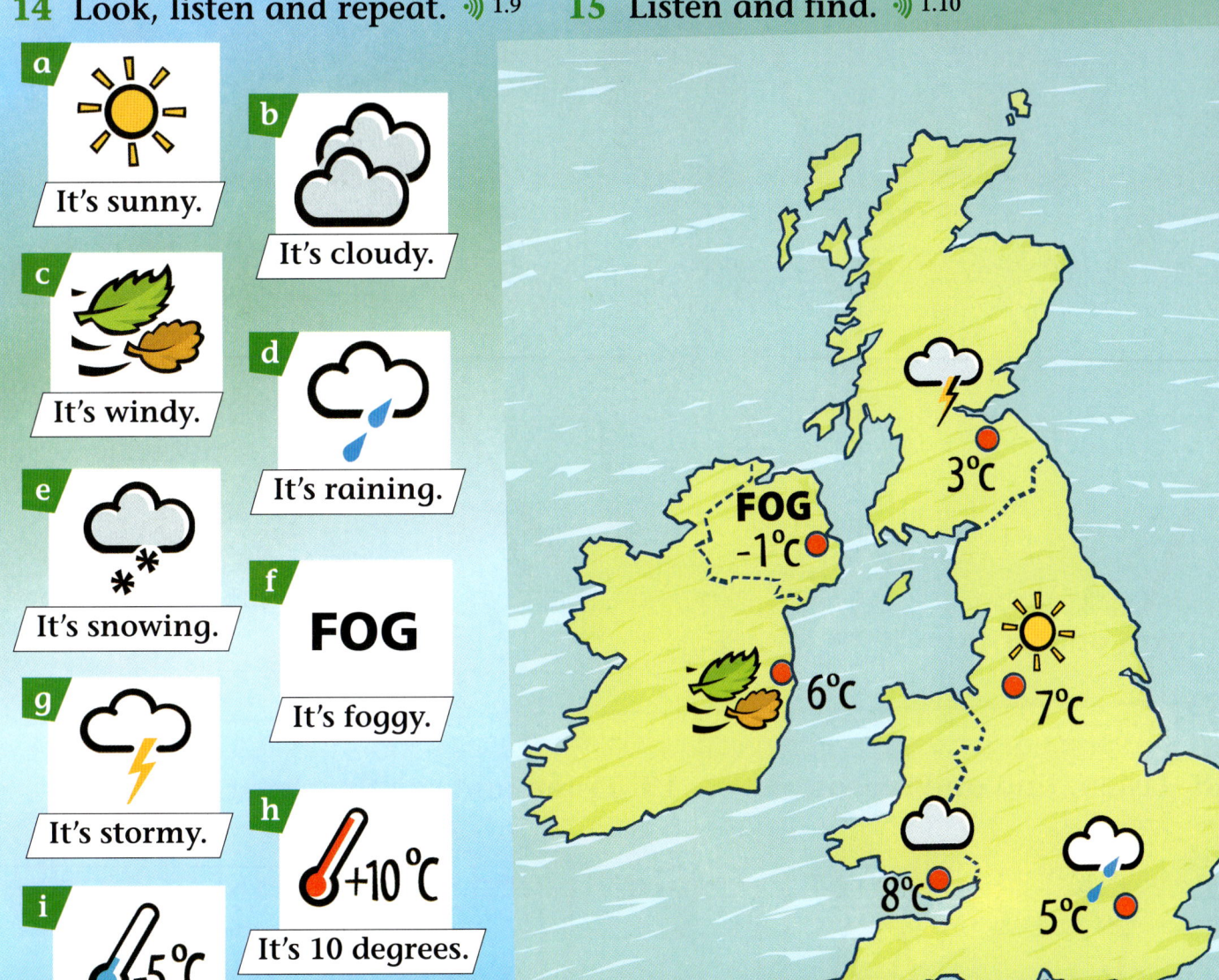

16 Ask and answer.

What's the weather like in Cardiff?

It's cloudy.

What's the weather like in Cardiff?

It's **sunny**.

It's **10 degrees**.

Manchester   Dublin
Edinburgh   Belfast   London

windy   snowing   raining
cloudy   stormy   foggy

minus 5

Geography

Unit 1　**9**

17 Make a weather map. PMB page 8

1 Draw and write.

2 Colour.

3 Write.

18 Listen, find and repeat. 1.11   **19** Listen and say the chant. 1.12

chant

| sk | sw | sn | sl | st |
| scooter | swing | snow | slide | standing |

Playing on a red swing,
Sliding down a slide,
Standing on a climbing frame
Up so high!

Playing on a scooter,
Skiing in the snow,
Swimming in the water,
Here we go!

10 Unit 1

Geography Pronunciation /sk/ /sw/ /sn/ /sl/ /st/

2 Art

1 Look, listen and repeat. 1.13   **2** Listen and find. 1.14

| 1 pirate | 2 astronaut | 3 teacher | 4 policeman | 5 footballer | 6 scientist |
| 7 actor | 8 pilot | 9 doctor | 10 dancer | 11 artist | 12 firefighter |

3 Ask and answer.

behind   next to
in front of   under   on

— Where's Luke?
— He's next to the footballer.

Jobs

Unit 2   11

5 Read and write *true* or *false*.

1. Eve's wearing a green jacket.
2. Archie hasn't got any paint.
3. Anna is a teacher.
4. Molly gets up at six o'clock.
5. Anna is late.
6. Anna falls off her bike.
7. Jazmin has an idea.
8. The children paint the bike.

6 Which sentence is in the story? Make more sentences. `PMB page 11`

7 Listen and say which picture. 🔊 1.17

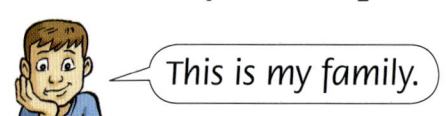

8 Play the game.

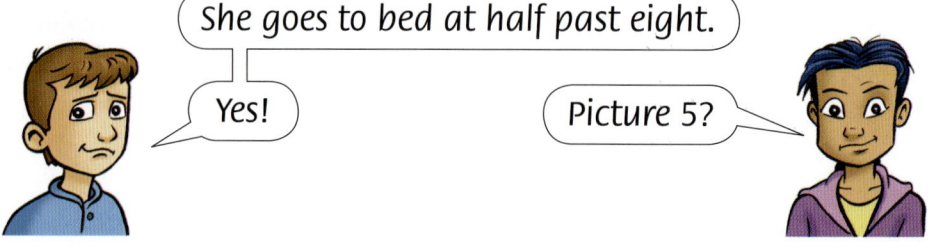

14 Unit 2 — She gets up / We get up at eight o'clock.

9 Read and write which club.   Notices

A Art Club
- Learn to paint, draw, and make models.
- Every Saturday morning at ten o'clock.

We've got paint, paper and pencils at the club but you need to bring an old shirt.

B Music Club

Every Saturday afternoon at 2 o'clock.

Learn to play a musical instrument!

We've got a piano, guitars, a flute and a xylophone.

C

- Do you want to act? Do you like singing and dancing? Or do you want to help with make-up? Come to **Drama Club**!
- Every Sunday afternoon at 2 o'clock.
- Learn from professional actor John May.

1 I want to learn to play the piano.
2 I want to sing.
3 I want to learn to make models.
4 I want to act.
5 I want to go to a club on Sunday.
6 I want to go to a club on Saturday afternoon.

10 Listen and read. Then sing the song. 1.19

We love painting pictures,
Red, yellow, blue and green.
We're good at painting pictures,
But not so good at staying clean!

Andy's got blue fingers,
Jenny's hair is green.
Let's tidy up and wash our hands,
Then we can have our tea!

Notices • Tidying up together

Drawing with a grid

Learn to copy pictures using a grid.

11 Look, listen and repeat. 🔊 1.20   **12** Listen and find. 🔊 1.21

a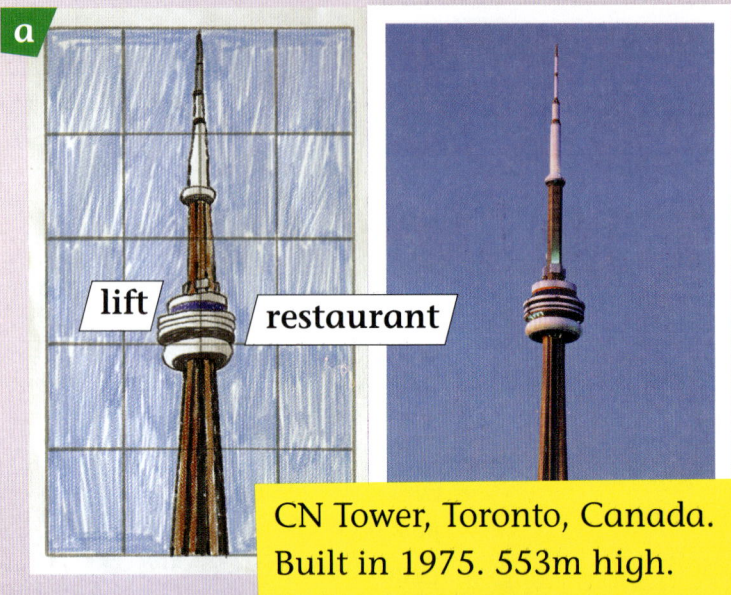
lift restaurant
CN Tower, Toronto, Canada. Built in 1975. 553m high.

b
stairs
Leaning tower of Pisa, Italy. Built 1173-1350. 55m high.

c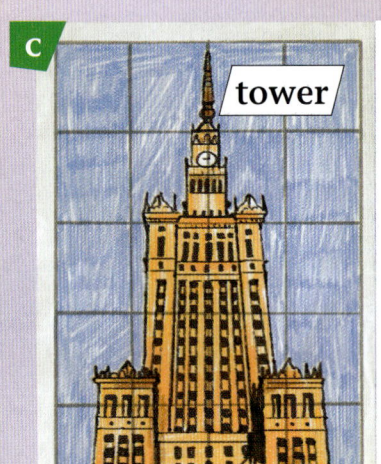
tower
Palace of Science and Culture, Warsaw, Poland. Built 1953-1955. 230m high.

d
clock
Big Ben, London, England. Built in 1858. 98m high.

13 Ask and answer.

— Tell me about this tower.

— It's 553 metres high. It's got a restaurant and a lift. It was built in 1975. It's in Canada. It's the CN Tower.

Talk about it!

It's **553** metres high.   230   55   98
It was built **in 1975**.   between 1173 and 1350
                            between 1953 and 1955
                            in 1858
It's in **Canada**.   Poland   England   Italy

16 Unit 2   Buildings

14 Look at the pictures. Read and order the texts to match the pictures.

15 Listen and check. 🔊 1.22

This is the Eiffel Tower in Paris, France. It was built in 1889. It's 329 metres high. It's got 1,665 steps, three lifts and two restaurants. You can see the whole of Paris from the top!

a When we finish all the squares we have a copy of the photo of the Eiffel Tower. ☐

b Now we copy the lines of the tower in each small square. ☐

c We want to make a drawing of the Eiffel Tower. This is a grid. It has got 20 squares. First we draw the grid onto the photo. ☐

d Now we draw the grid onto a blank piece of paper. If we want to make our picture bigger than the photo, we draw a bigger grid. ☐

Art

Unit 2 · 17

16 Copy a drawing with a grid. PMB page 13

1 Draw a grid on the picture.
2 Copy the grid.
3 Copy the picture.
4 Colour and write.

17 Listen, find and repeat. 1.23   **18** Listen and say the chant. 1.24

ə 
doctor

Soldier, sailor,
Singer, dancer,
Policeman,
Postman,
Fireman,
Chief!

Doctor, actor,
Pilot, pirate,
Policeman,
Postman,
Fireman,
Chief!

chant

3 Health

1 Look, listen and repeat. 1.25   **2** Listen and find. 1.26

I feel …
1 dizzy. 2 sick.

I've got … 3 a headache. 4 a cough. 5 a cold. 6 a sore throat.
7 a toothache. 8 an earache. 9 a stomach ache.

3 Ask and answer.

What's the matter?

I've got a headache.

Oh dear!

Health

Unit 3 19

The TV show

You should sit still. You shouldn't eat so many sweets!

5 Match.

1 The children are travelling in
2 Molly is eating a lot of
3 Archie has got
4 Molly is feeling
5 Suzy Silver has a problem with her
6 The children are sitting at
7 Eve is feeling

a a headache.
b the club car.
c sick.
d sweets.
e dizzy.
f van.
g the front of the concert.

Unit 3 **21**

6 Which sentence is in the story? Make more sentences. PMB page 16

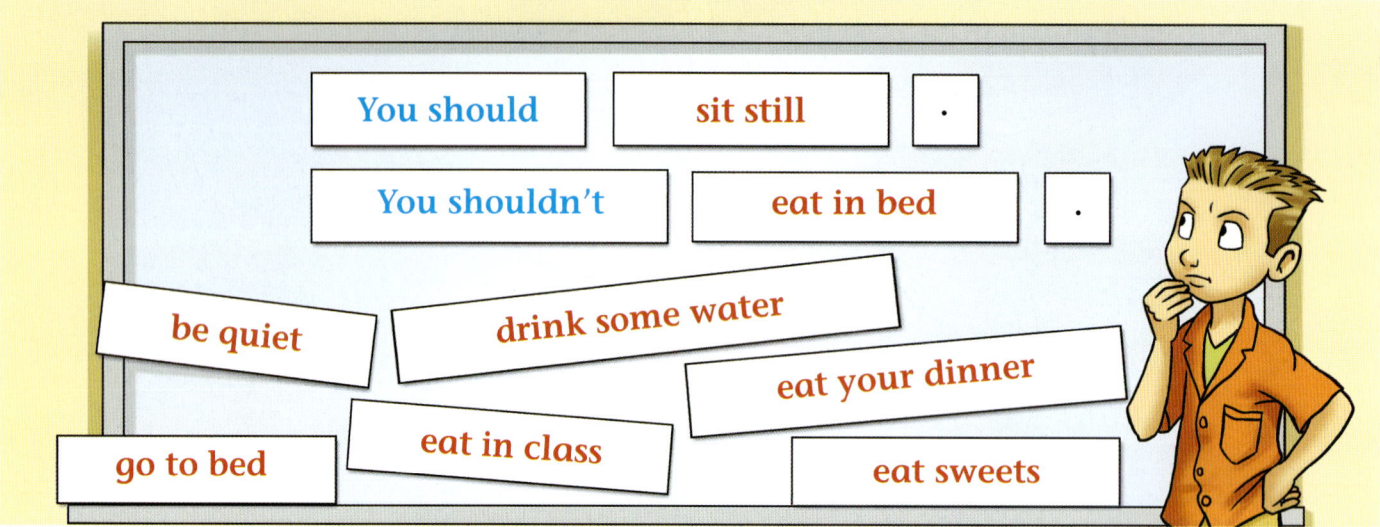

7 Listen and say which picture. 1.29

8 Play the game.

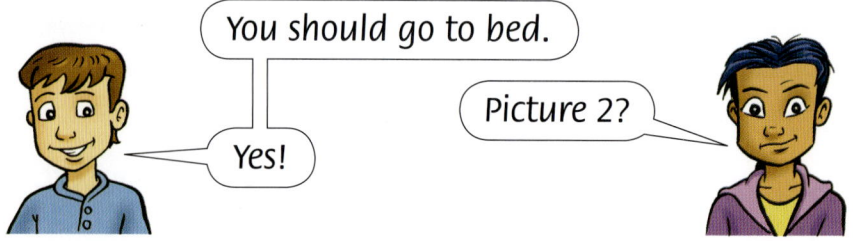

You should go to bed.
Yes!
Picture 2?

22 Unit 3

You should sit still. You shouldn't eat sweets.

9 Read and find the pictures. Then read and write *true* or *false*.   Posters

4 rules for healthy children

a

Your health is very important! You need exercise and healthy food and lots of sleep. Here are the rules to keep you healthy!

b

1 You should eat lots of fruit and vegetables – at least 5 portions a day. You shouldn't eat lots of junk food. Hamburgers and chips are nice for a special treat, but not for every day.

2 You should drink lots of water. Don't drink lots of fizzy drinks.

d

3 You should sleep for 8 hours every night. Go to bed early so you can wake up easily.

4 You should exercise every day. You can run, walk, go swimming, play football or skip with your friends – it's all good for you!

1 You should eat junk food.
2 Fizzy drinks are good for you.
3 Lots of sleep is good for you.
4 You shouldn't exercise every day.

10 Listen and read. Then sing the song. 1.31

song

Apples in the morning,
Bananas all the time.
Fruit will give you energy,
It helps you run and climb.

Swimming in the morning,
Basketball at night.
Exercise will make you fit,
It keeps you strong and bright!

Posters • Living healthily

Unit 3 | 23

Pulse rates

Learn about pulse rates and how to take your pulse.

11 Look, listen and repeat. 🔊 1.32

12 Listen, read and answer. 🔊 1.33

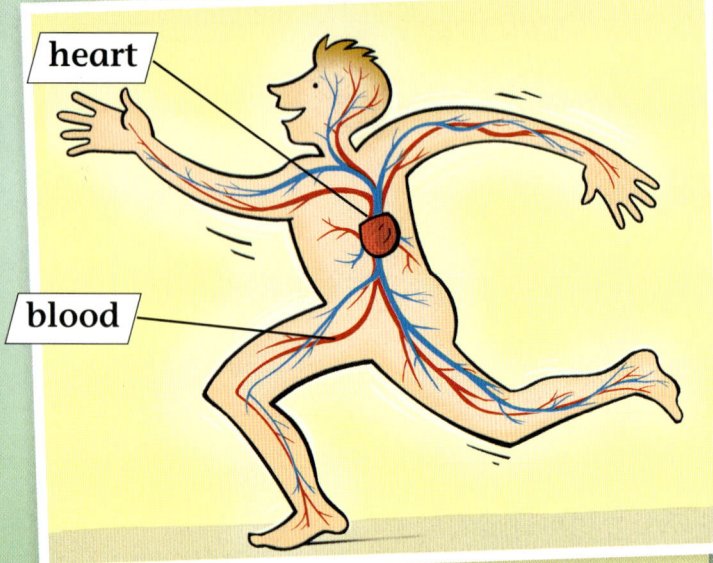

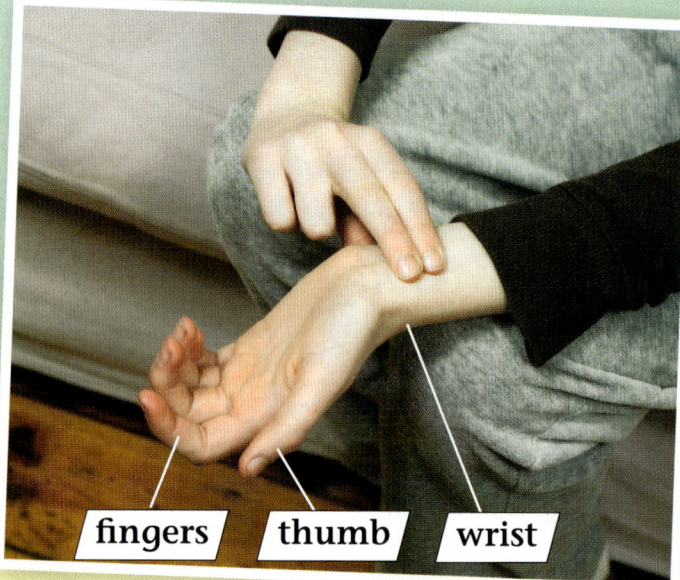

Your heart pumps blood around your body. Your heart usually beats about 70 times per minute. When you do a lot of exercise, your heart works more and so it beats more.

You can feel these heartbeats. Put two fingers under the thumb on your left wrist. Press your wrist gently with your fingers. This is your pulse. You measure your pulse in beats per minute (BPM). Take your pulse for 10 seconds. How many beats? Now multiply this number by 6. How many beats per minute is your pulse?

13 Read and match.

Time	7.00	7.30	8.00
A	150 BPM	70 BPM	100 BPM
B	70 BPM	75 BPM	80 BPM
C	65 BPM	70 BPM	150 BPM

1 Olga gets up early and goes running at seven o'clock. Then at 7.30 she has breakfast and watches TV. At eight o'clock she goes to school. She walks to school.

2 Milly reads in bed at seven o'clock. She gets up and has breakfast at 7.30. At eight o'clock she runs to school. She's always late!

3 Josh has breakfast at seven o'clock. At 7.30 he gets dressed. At eight o'clock he takes the bus to school.

14 Listen and find. 🔊 1.34

1 68 BPM

2 97 BPM

3 140 BPM

4 120 BPM

5 89 BPM

6 78 BPM

15 Ask and answer.

What's her pulse after playing football?

It's 120.

Talk about it!

What's her pulse after **sleeping**?

playing football?
walking to school?
skipping?
playing computer games?
reading?

It's **68**.

97   140   120   89   78

Science

16 Make a BPM chart. PMB page 18

1 Take your pulse.

2 Do the activity for one minute.

3 Take your pulse again. Write.

17 Listen, find and repeat. 1.35   **18** Listen and say the chant. 1.36

[tʃ] chicken

[ʃ] shoes

chant

It's party time, so wash your hands.
We're eating in the kitchen.
Come on, children,
Hurry up!
There's fish and chips and chicken!

Take off your shoes and find a chair,
And choose the dish for you.
There's fish and chips
And chicken and chips,
And chocolate cheesecake too!

4 On the farm

1 Look, listen and repeat. 1.37 **2** Listen and find. 1.38

1 grass   2 weeds   3 water   4 goat   5 peppers   6 tomatoes
7 onions   8 strawberries   9 cauliflower   10 beans   11 potatoes   12 milk

3 Ask and answer.

water
eat
drink

What's Molly doing?

She's watering the tomatoes.

Farming

Unit 4 27

Helping on the farm

There's some water.

5 Read and find the picture.

a Eve shows Finn the water.
b Finn picks the beans.
c Eve arrives.
d Eve laughs.
e Archie's T-shirt is wet.
f Eve gives jobs to the children.
g The goat is escaping.
h Finn falls over Coco.

Unit 4 29

6 Which sentence is in the story? Make more sentences. PMB page 21

7 Listen and say which picture. 1.41

8 Play the game.

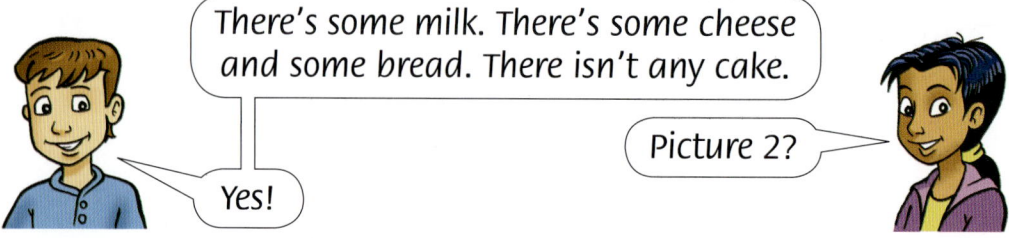

30 Unit 4   There's some milk. There isn't any cheese.

9 Read. Then look at the pictures and write the day.   Notes

Hi Eve,
Thanks for your help while I'm on holiday. There are some important jobs on the farm.

Monday
Please water the beans. They need a lot of water.

Tuesday
Pick some peppers. Please put them on the kitchen table.

Wednesday
Please water the tomatoes.

Thursday
Pick some tomatoes. Please put them next to the peppers on the table.

Friday
Pick some strawberries. You can take some home to your family.

Every day
Don't forget to give some water to the goat every day.

Thank you!
See you in 2 weeks,
Pam

PS There's a cake in the cupboard for you – I hope you like it!

10 Listen and read. Then sing the song. 🔊 1.43

We plant the beans and onions,
We plant the pepper seeds,
We plant them all and let them grow,
But watch out for the weeds!

We water them in summer,
We need both rain and sun,
We pick them when they're ready,
Then eat them – yum, yum, yum!

How plants grow

Learn about plants: their food and habitats

11 Look and read.   **12** Listen, read and answer. 1.44

There are thousands of different types of plants. Some grow in hot, dry deserts. Can you think of a plant that grows in the desert?
Some plants grow in cold, wet forests. Some grow under the ice and snow! Do you know any plants that grow in cold places?
Plants can make their own food. This process is called photosynthesis. They need air, water, and sunlight. The plants take a gas called carbon dioxide from the air and water from the rain. Then they use the sunlight to produce oxygen. The oxygen goes back into the air. The plants change the carbon dioxide and water into food. This food is very sugary. It is called sap. This all happens in the leaves of the plant. The sap then travels from the leaves into the stem. Then it can go to where the plant needs food.

13 Read and write *true* or *false*.

1 Plants can grow when it is hot.
2 Plants can't grow when it is very cold.
3 Plants need sunlight to make food.
4 Sap is sugary.
5 The sap begins in the stems.

14 Look listen and repeat. 🔊 1.45   **15** Look, listen and find. 🔊 1.46

sunflowers — hot — sunny

pine trees — needles — wet — cold — dry

cacti — spikes

palm trees — leaves

ferns — shady

Talk about it!

16 Ask and answer.

- Tell me about a plant.
- Sunflowers grow in hot, sunny places. They've got big, yellow flowers.

They grow in **hot, sunny places**.   wet   shady
                                      cold   dry

They've got **big, yellow flowers**.   leaves   spikes
                                        needles

Science   Unit 4   **33**

17 Make a plant table. PMB page 23

1 Draw and colour. 2 Tick. 3 Write.

18 Listen, find and repeat. 1.47   **19** Listen and say the chant. 1.48

chant

əʊ goat

æ cat

40 goats,
50 cats,
60 coats,
70 hats,
80 boats,
90 rats,
And one hundred acrobats!

Science Pronunciation [əʊ] [æ]

5 Animal life

1 Look, listen and repeat. 2.1 **2** Listen and find. 2.2

| 1 tall | 2 fast | 3 big | 4 strong | 5 thin |
| 6 fat | 7 hungry | 8 long | 9 short | 10 slow | 11 small |

3 Ask and answer.

tortoise lion elephant
snake zebra crocodile
bee cheetah giraffe

— It's small. It's slow.
— Is it the tortoise?
— Yes, it is.

Adjectives of appearance

Unit 5 **35**

The new cat

5 Read and write *true* or *false*.

1 The mice eat the food in the club.
2 The new cat is big.
3 Molly likes the new cat.
4 Coco likes the new cat.
5 The new cat takes Coco's bed.
6 The new cat is fast.
7 Coco is fast.
8 Coco catches a mouse.

6 Which sentence is in the story? Make more sentences. PMB page 26

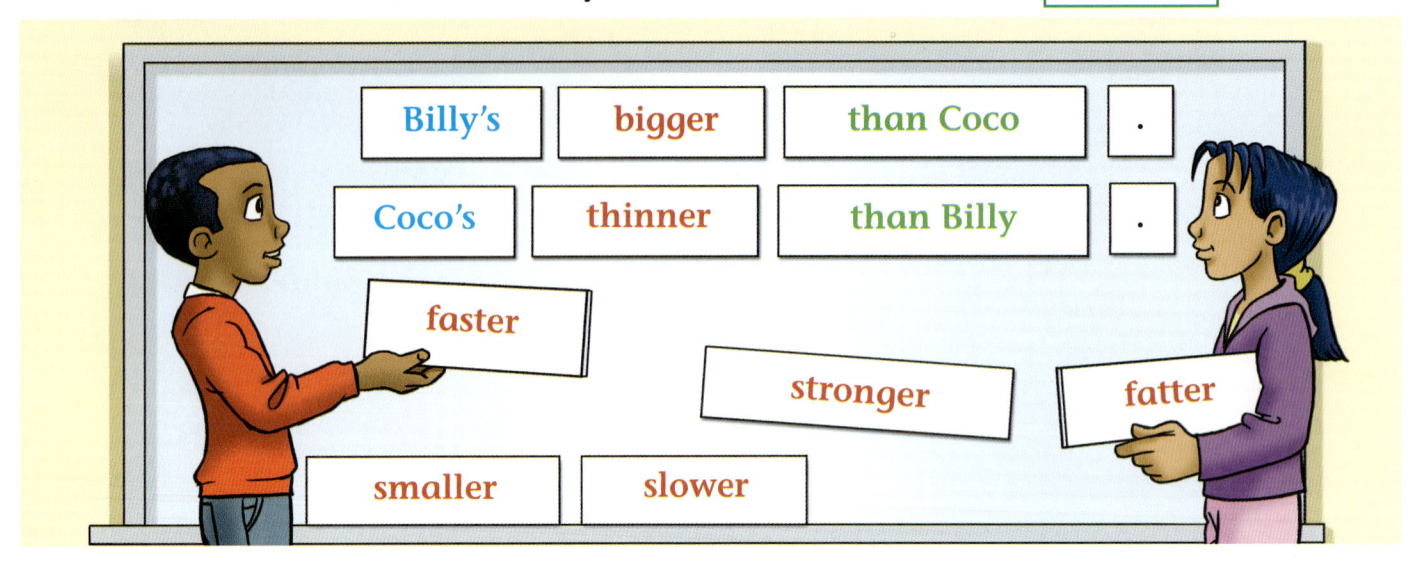

Billy's — bigger — than Coco — .
Coco's — thinner — than Billy — .
faster
stronger
fatter
smaller — slower

7 Listen and say which picture. 2.5

1
2
3
4
5
6

8 Ask and answer.

The lion is stronger than the mouse.
Yes!
Picture 4?

38 Unit 5   The lion's stronger than the mouse.

9 Read and find the picture. Then write the animals.

Websites

1. This animal lives in India and Africa. The African animal has bigger ears than the Indian animal. It eats leaves. It needs lots of food because it's very big. Sometimes people ride on this animal. It is usually grey.

2. This animal is very big – it's the biggest animal in the world. It lives in the sea. It can swim under water for a long time, but it needs to come up for air. It can eat three tonnes of food every day. It eats by opening its mouth as it swims. This animal is grey and blue.

3. This animal eats small insects. It lives in houses and in gardens. Some are very small but some are quite big. It can move quite fast. It isn't an insect. It's got eight legs. Some people are very frightened of this animal.

spider

elephant

blue whale

1 It lives in the sea.
2 It can move fast.
3 It eats plants.
4 It's got big ears.
5 It can be very small.
6 It eats insects.

10 Listen and read. Then sing the song. 2.7

song

The crocodile lives in the river,
The monkey lives in the trees,
But we're taking all of their water,
And chopping down all of their trees.

Save them, save them, oh save all the animals
Please, oh please!

So let's work together to save them,
Let's go and plant hundreds of trees,
Let's stop wasting all of our water,
Let's save all the animals, please!

Save them …

Websites   Protecting wildlife

Bees

Learn about bees and their habits

11 Look, listen and repeat. 🔊 2.8   **12** Listen, read and answer. 🔊 2.9

beehive

worker

comb

honey

Honey bees are social insects. There are different types of bees – drones, workers and queen bees. They live together in a beehive.

The work in a beehive is divided beween the bees. The queen is the biggest bee in the colony. She is the only bee that lays eggs. Sometimes a queen can lay 3,000 eggs in a single day. Can you find the queen in this picture?

Worker bees are female but do not lay eggs. A colony can have 50,000 to 60,000 workers. Workers give food to the queen and babies. They clean the hive. Some workers build the comb and store the food. Older workers collect the food from the flowers and make the honey. What is the worker bee doing in this picture?

People collect the combs from the beehive. They put the honey in jars and we eat it – yum! Can you see the comb in this jar?

Drones are male bees. They have very big eyes. Look at this drone. Look at his eyes. Drones don't collect food from flowers or work in the hive. But life isn't all good! When there isn't enough food or when it's cold the workers push them out of the hive and they die.

queen

drone

13 Read and answer.

Queen, drone or worker?
1. This bee lays eggs.
2. This bee cleans the hive.
3. This bee collects the food.
4. This bee doesn't work.
5. This bee makes honey.
6. This bee is bigger than the others.

14 Listen and find. 🔊 2.10

a b c d e

Talk about it!

15 Ask and answer.

Tell me about this bee.

It's female. It lays eggs. It's the queen.

It's **female**.   male
It **collects food**.   gives food to the queen
cleans the hive   doesn't work very hard
makes the comb   makes honey
lays eggs   has got big eyes
It's **a worker**.   the queen   a drone

Science

Unit 5 | **41**

16 Make a bee diagram. PMB page 28

1 Draw and colour.

2 Write.

17 Listen, find and repeat. 2.11   **18** Listen and say the chant. 2.12

ə

fast**er**

chant

I'm bigg**er** than my sist**er**,
But small**er** than my mum.
I'm fast**er** than my broth**er**,
Especially when we run!

I'm strong**er** than my cousin,
But weak**er** than my dad.
I'm fast**er** than my broth**er**,
Especially when I'm bad!

6 Safety

1 Look, listen and repeat. 2.13   **2** Listen and find. 2.14

| 1 go right | 2 stop | 3 go left | 4 traffic lights | 5 car | 6 road |
| 7 zebra crossing | 8 sign | 9 bike | 10 helmet | 11 gloves |

3 Ask and answer.

> Start at the traffic lights. Go left at the stop sign. Go left again. Where are you?

> I'm behind the car.

Road safety

Unit 6 43

At the bike track

1
- Look, there's the track.
- Brilliant! Let's go.
- I love cycling down hills!
- Me, too!
- Stop! Safety first. Listen to me!

2
- You must wear a helmet.
- Yes, yes, we know. Can we go now?
- Let's go!

3
- I want to start!
- You can't go yet. Listen to me first.
- Me too!

4
- You mustn't ride into the bushes. You must watch out for the trees and stay on the path.
- Oh all right …

5
- And you mustn't ride in the water… aah!

You must wear a helmet. You mustn't ride in the water.

6

Watch out for the trees!

Oh no! The bushes! Watch out, Luke! Be careful!

He's in the water!

7 Oh no!

8 Look out! Be careful! Oh no!

9 OK, OK! You mustn't do that!

5 Read and write *true* or *false*.

1 Molly likes cycling down hills.
2 Luke wants the children to wear a helmet.
3 Archie wants to start.
4 Molly wants to listen.
5 Luke stays on the path.
6 Luke rides into the water.
7 Luke wants the children to ride into the water.

6 Which sentence is in the story? Make more sentences. PMB page 31

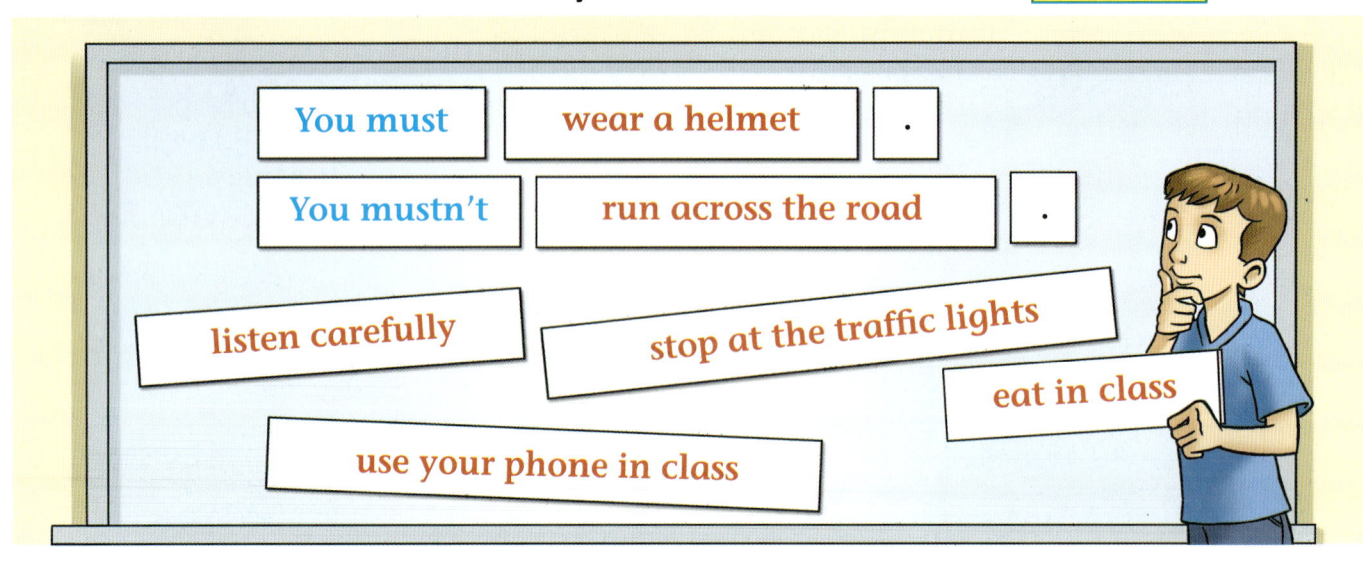

You must — wear a helmet .

You mustn't — run across the road .

listen carefully

stop at the traffic lights

eat in class

use your phone in class

7 Listen and say which picture. 2.18

1

2

3

4

5

8 Play the game.

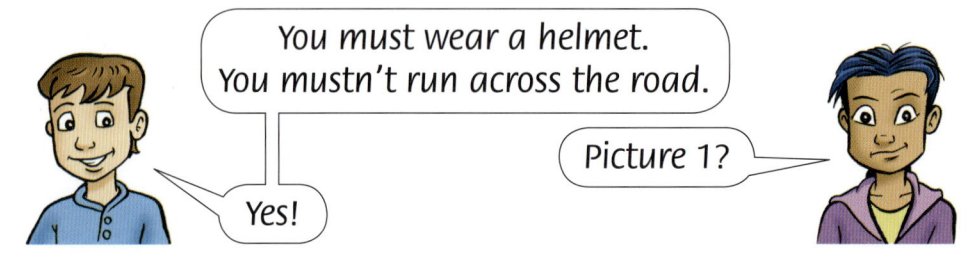

You must wear a helmet.
You mustn't run across the road.

Yes!

Picture 1?

46 Unit 6

You must listen carefully. You mustn't eat in class.

9 Read and match. Then look at the pictures and write the rule. **Signs**

1
WELCOME TO THE PARK!

We want to protect the park and make it a safe place. There are some rules you must follow.

1. You mustn't drive a car in the park.
2. You mustn't pick the flowers.
3. You mustn't ride your bike in the water.
4. You mustn't feed the ducks.
5. You mustn't fish.
6. You must put litter in the bin.

2 Look after our bike track!
1. You must wear a helmet.
2. You must stay on the path.
3. You mustn't ride in the river.
4. You mustn't drop litter.

3 Middleton Swimming Pool
1. You mustn't jump in the pool – it can be dangerous.
2. Wear a swimming hat in the big pool.
3. Listen to the lifeguards – they are here to help you.
4. You mustn't run – this is very dangerous.
5. You mustn't eat in the pool.

a b c d e f

10 Listen and read. Then sing the song. 2.20 **song**

Look left, look right,
Cross at the lights.
Green light, red,
Use your head!

Have a great time on your bike.
Go fast or slow, as you like.
Wear your helmet, use your light,
Enjoy the ride, but hold on tight!

Look left, look right …

Signs   Road safety

Unit 6

Speed

Learn to talk about speed in kilometres per hour.

11 Look, listen and repeat. 2.21

12 Listen, read and answer. 2.22

How do you go to school each day? Do you walk? Do you ride your bike or go by bus? Do you go by car? How far do you travel? How long does it take?

We measure speed in kilometres per hour. In many towns in Europe, the speed limit is 50 kilometres per hour (km/h). On many motorways the speed limit is 120 kilometres per hour.

Road signs show the speed limit. How fast can you travel if you see this sign?

This is a speedometer. You can see it in a car. It tells you how fast the car is travelling. How fast is this car travelling?

This is the fastest car in the world. It can travel at 1,228 kilometres per hour!

To calculate speed, we use the distance-speed-time triangle.

D = distance, S = speed, T = time

To calculate speed, you divide distance by time. For example, a car travels 80km in 2 hours. $\frac{80}{2}$ = 40. So the car is travelling at 40 km/h.

13 Read and answer.

1 What's the speed limit in many towns in Europe?
2 What's the speed limit on many motorways?
3 How fast can the fastest car travel?
4 How do we calculate speed?

14 Listen and match. 2.23

1 A person can walk at about
2 A car in town can travel at 
3 A cheetah can run at 
4 A racing car can travel at 
5 A plane can travel at 
6 A space shuttle can travel at 

a 1000 km/h
b 6 km/h
c 360 km/h
d 100 km/h
e 50 km/h
f 26,000 km/h

Talk about it!

15 Ask and answer.

How fast can a racing car travel?
360 kilometres per hour.

How fast can a racing car   travel?   360 km/h.
               a car in town
               a plane
               a space shuttle

               a person   walk?
               a cheetah   run?

Maths

Unit 6   49

16 Make a scale. PMB page 33

1 Draw and colour.

2 Write.

17 Listen, find and repeat. 2.24

18 Listen and say the chant. 2.25

chant

k — cake

s — cycling

There's a circus in the city.
In the circus, there's a clown.
He likes cakes and he likes cycling,
And he wears a funny crown!

He's a clown,
A cycling clown,
He eats cakes and wears a crown!

He's a clown,
A cycling clown,
He's a crazy, cycling clown!

Maths • Pronunciation [k] [s]

7 At school

1 Look, listen and repeat. 2.26   **2** Listen and find. 2.27

1 Maths   2 History   3 Geography   4 Art   5 Science   6 P.E.
7 Spanish   8 Music   9 English   10 classroom   11 poster

3 Ask and answer.

Do you like Maths?   Yes, I do.

Do you like Music?   No, I don't.

School

Unit 7   51

The good old days

1 It's Sports Day at school...

— Come on, Dad. We mustn't be late.
— OK, I'm coming...oh look, there's my old teacher!

2
— Were you good at school?
— I was good at History. My favourite topic was Ancient Egypt. I wasn't very good at Maths.

3
— There weren't any calculators or computers.
— Really?

4
— What about school lunches, Dad?
— Oh, they were terrible.

5 The teachers were very strict when I was a boy.

6
— Was there a Sports Day, Dad? Were you good at P.E.?
— Yes, there was. I was very good at P.E.!

I was good at History. I wasn't good at Maths.

7 I won a medal!

Wow! That's great, Dad!

8 Hello, young man.

Hello. I'm telling Finn and Jazmin about my medal at Sports Day.

9 Ah yes, the medal! That was a good day for you.

10 You were the only runner! Everybody was sick.

It's true! I was good at sports, but I was also very lucky!

5 Read and write *true* or *false*.

1. It's Art Day at school.
2. Finn's dad sees his old teacher.
3. The teacher is an old man now.
4. Finn's dad was good at Maths.
5. Finn's dad had a calculator at school.
6. School lunches were great.
7. Finn's dad got a medal.
8. There were lots of other children in the race.

6 Which sentence is in the story? Make more sentences. PMB page 36

- I was · good at History .
- I wasn't · good at Science .
- She was · good at Art
- He wasn't · good at Maths
- He was · She wasn't

7 Listen and say who. 2.31

	Jazmin's Mum	Eve's Mum	Finn's Dad	Teacher	Archie's Dad
Maths	✓	✓	✗	✓	✓
Science	✓	✗	✓	✗	✓
Art	✗	✓	✓	✓	✗

8 Play the game.

She was good at Maths and Art. She wasn't good at Science.
Yes!
Eve's mum?

He was good at Science. He wasn't good at Art.

9 Read and match. Answer the questions.

Fact files

Middleton Primary School Magazine

I'm Luke. I love History and Art. I want to be an artist when I grow up. I do lots of sport, but my favourite sport is basketball. I like animals too – I've got a cat and I really like big cats like cheetahs.

Hi, I'm Jazmin. My favourite subject is Science – I want to be a scientist when I grow up. I like playing tennis too. I'm also good at Maths, but I'm not very good at Art.

Hi, I'm John. I was a student at this school 20 years ago, and now my son is a student here! I liked running but I wasn't very good at it! My favourite subject was Art. I was good at Geography and Art, but I wasn't very good at Maths.

My name's Finn. I like Art the best, but I like Geography too. I'm not very good at Science. My favourite sport is running. My dad was at this school too when he was a boy.

1 Name: _____
Sports: running
Favourite subject: Art
Good at: Art and Geography
Not good at: Science
Interesting fact: father was a student at this school

2 Name: _____
Sports: tennis
Favourite subject: Science
Good at: Maths and Science
Not good at: Art
Interesting fact: wants to be a scientist

3 Name: _____
Sports: basketball
Favourite subject: History
Good at: History and Art
Not good at: Maths
Interesting fact: favourite animal is a cheetah

4 Name: _____
Sports: running
Favourite subject: Art
Good at: Geography and Art
Not good at: Maths
Interesting fact: son is now at the school

1 Who wants to be a scientist?
2 Who was at the school 20 years ago?
3 Who likes animals?
4 Who likes Geography?

10 Listen and read. Then sing the song. 2.33

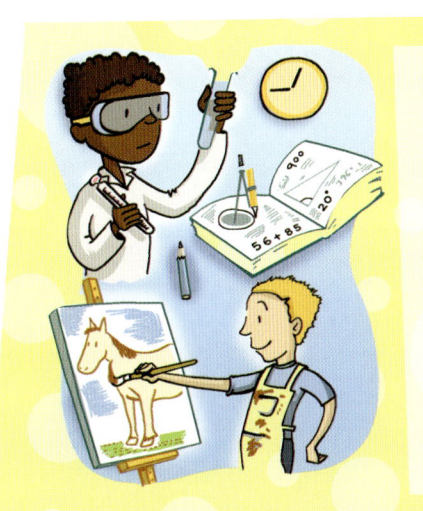

song

Science is at nine o'clock,
Geography's at ten,
Half an hour for break time,
And then there's class again.

I like Maths and History,
My favourite class is Art,
No matter what the subject,
We study very hard!

Fact files • Working hard at school

Unit 7 **55**

Ancient Egypt

Learn about the culture of Ancient Egypt.

11 Look, listen and repeat. 2.34

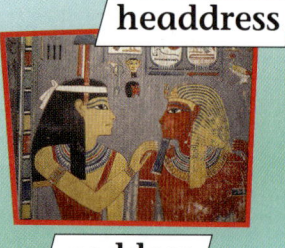

mummy — pyramid — god — pharaoh — goddess — headdress

12 Listen, read and answer. 2.35

The River Nile was very important in Ancient Egypt. The Nile is the longest river in the world: it is 6,695 kilometres long. The Ancient Egyptians lived next to the River Nile because the land was good for farming. Can you find the river?

Pharaohs were kings in Ancient Egypt. When they died, the people buried them in tombs. The Ancient Egyptians built pyramids as tombs for the pharaohs and their queens. The three biggest pyramids are at Giza. Can you find Giza on the map?

When pharaohs or other important people died, their bodies were wrapped in special bandages. A body wrapped and buried like this is called a mummy. They last for thousands of years.

The Ancient Egyptians believed in many different gods and goddesses. Each god or goddess was very important in Ancient Egypt. Sometimes the god or goddess had the head of an animal. Can you see a god or goddess with the head of an animal on this page?

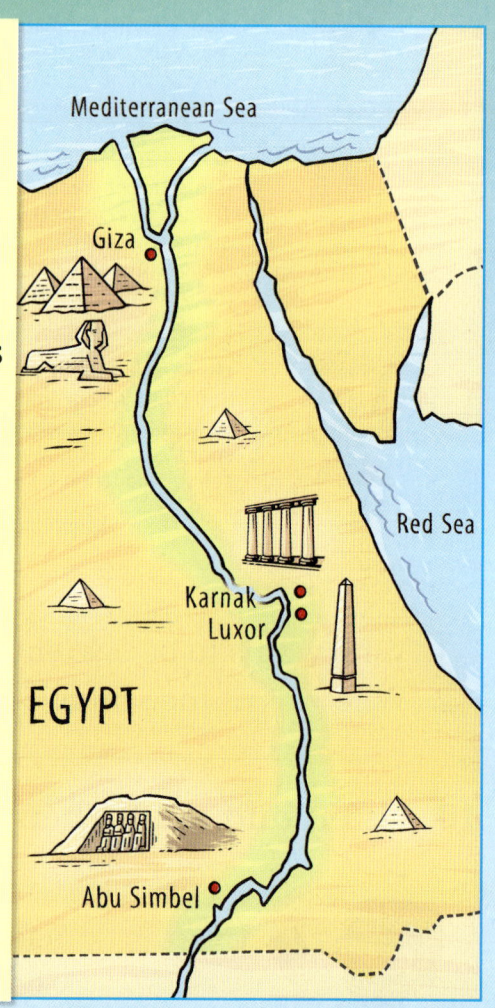

13 Read and write *true* or *false*.

1. The River Nile is 6,695 km long.
2. The Nile was important because the land was good for farming.
3. The Pharaoh was the queen of Ancient Egypt.
4. The biggest pyramids are at Giza.
5. The mummies weren't important people.

14 Listen and find. 🔊 2.36

a Osiris was the god of the dead. He was the father of Horus. He had a white headdress with feathers.

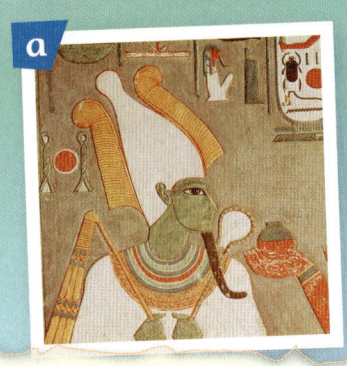

b Horus was a god of the sky. He was the son of Isis and Osiris. He had the head of a bird.

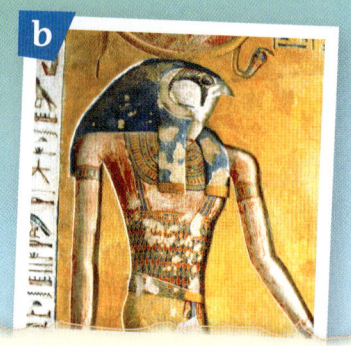

c Isis was the mother goddess. She was the wife of Osiris and the mother of Horus. She had a headdress of cow horns.

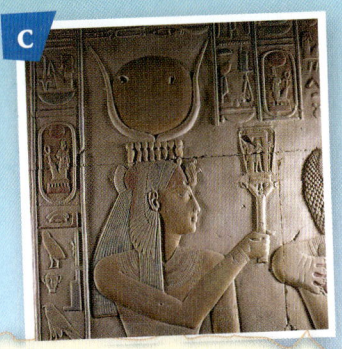

d Sobek was a god of the Nile. He had the head of a crocodile and a headdress of feathers.

e Bastet was a goddess with the head of a cat. She was a kind goddess. Cats were very important in Ancient Egypt.

f Tefnut was the goddess of water. She had the head of a lioness.

15 Ask and answer.

- Is it a god? — Yes.
- Did he have the head of a bird? — No.
- Did he have a headdress of white feathers? — Yes.
- Osiris! — Yes!

Talk about it!

Is it a **god**?   goddess?
Did he/she have   **the head of a lioness?**
the head of a crocodile?
the head of a cat?
the head of a bird?

a headdress with feathers?
a headdress with cow horns?

History   Unit 7   57

16 Make Egyptian pictures. PMB page 38

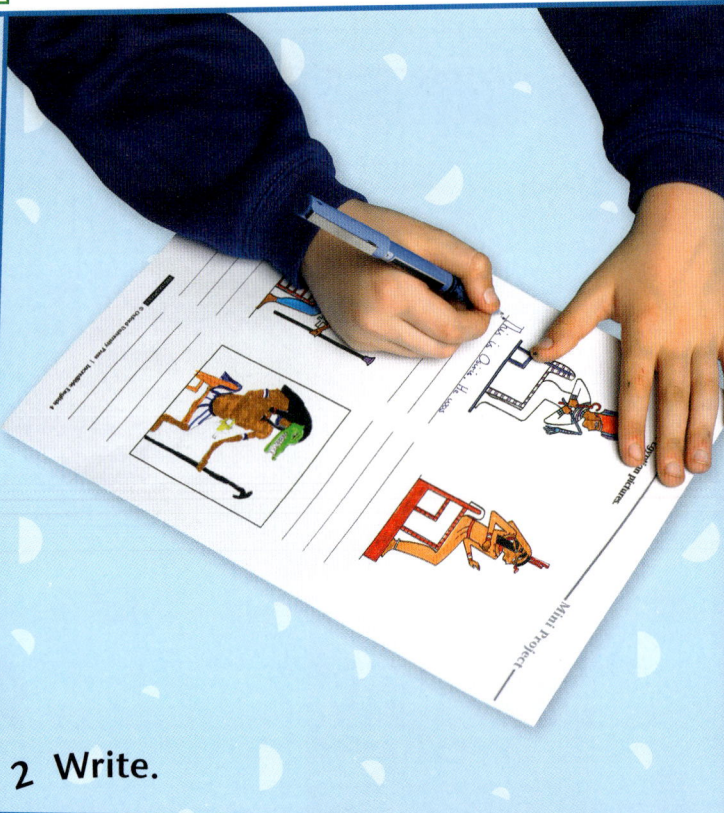

1 Draw and colour.

2 Write.

17 Listen, find and repeat. 2.37   **18** Listen and say the chant. 2.38

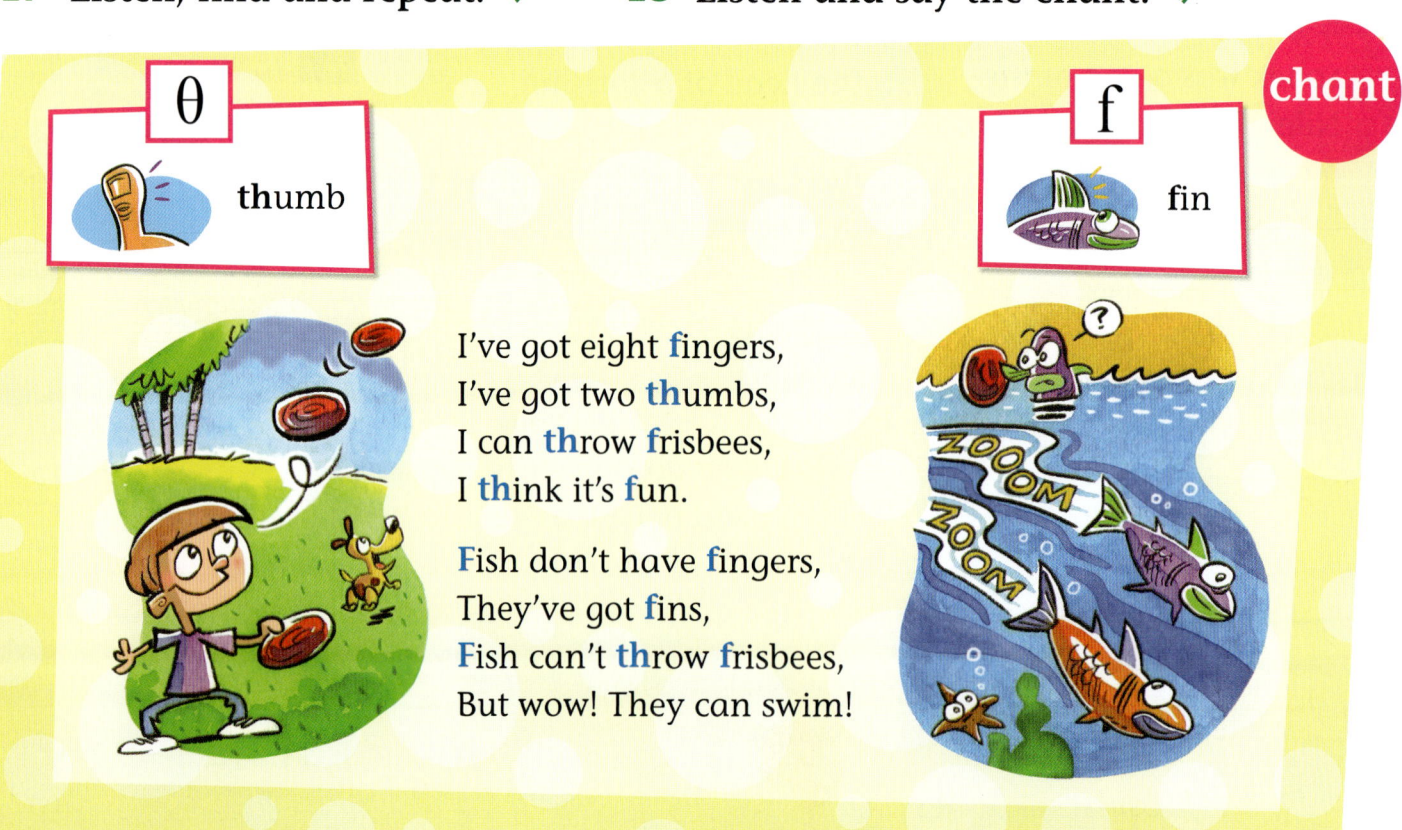

chant

θ thumb

f fin

I've got eight **f**ingers,
I've got two **th**umbs,
I can **th**row **f**risbees,
I **th**ink it's **f**un.

Fish don't have **f**ingers,
They've got **f**ins,
Fish can't **th**row **f**risbees,
But wow! They can swim!

58 Unit 7 · History · Pronunciation [θ] [f]

8 Underwater life

1 Look, listen and repeat. 2.39   **2** Listen and find. 2.40

| 1 water | 2 boat | 3 shark | 4 dolphin | 5 jellyfish | 6 fish |
| 7 octopus | 8 seahorse | 9 crab | 10 starfish | 11 shell | 12 sand |

3 Ask and answer.

How many sharks are there?   There are two.

Sea life

Unit 8 59

At Water World

1. We went to Water World. We had a great time!

2. Did you see lots of fish?
Yes. I saw an octopus, a jellyfish, a seahorse and lots of fish!

3. And Coco saw the fish too …

4. At lunchtime we had egg and chips … and we all had chocolate ice creams.
But Coco wanted to eat the fish!

5. And she fell in!

6. And then we saw a shark! We were really scared, and Coco was, too.

I saw an octopus. I had egg and chips for lunch.

5 Read and find the picture.

a Coco falls in the water.
b The children have lunch.
c Coco has fish for lunch.
d The children come home from Water World.
e The children see a jellyfish.
f The children see an octopus.
g Coco swims with the dolphin.

6 Which sentence is in the story? Make more sentences. PMB page 41

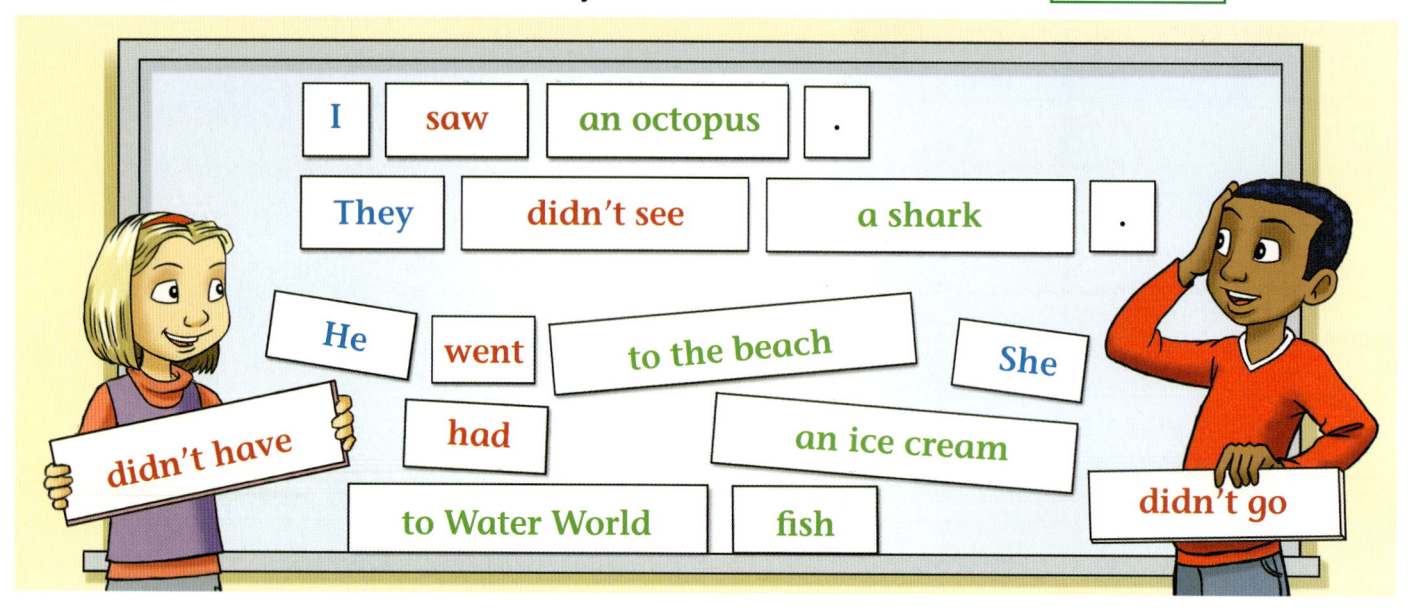

I	saw	an octopus	.
They	didn't see	a shark	.
He	went	to the beach	She
didn't have	had	an ice cream	didn't go
	to Water World	fish	

7 Listen and say which picture. 2.44

1
2
3
4
5
6

8 Play the game.

She saw a shark.
She didn't see a starfish.

Picture 5.

Yes!

62 Unit 8

She saw a shark. She didn't see a starfish.

9 Read and write *true* or *false*.

Leaflets

Come to Water World!

Every day we learn more and more about the amazing world of the sea. At Water World you can see this wonderful world!

Did you know …
- the highest mountain in the world is under the sea?
- there are more than 29,000 species of fish?
- the biggest animal in the world lives in the sea?
- the deepest part of the sea is over 10km deep?

At Water World you can walk in our underwater tunnels and see fish swim past your nose! You can see sharks, crabs, jellyfish and lots more!

In the outdoor pools you can watch our dolphins jumping and playing.

In the Water World Shop you can buy Water World DVDs, posters of your favourite fish, and more Water World souvenirs.

And don't forget about food! In the Water World Café and Restaurant we have delicious hot and cold food for you! You can have fish and chips, sandwiches and ice cream.

Come to Water World today!

1 At Water World you can learn about mountains under the sea.
2 At Water World you can see jellyfish.
3 You can learn to swim at Water World.
4 At Water World you can't buy posters.
5 There isn't a café at Water World.

10 Listen and read. Then sing the song. 2.46

song

We're going to the beach, hurray!
We're going to the sea!

Let's pack our bags, what do we need?
Shorts and towels and strong suncream,
And games to play for you and me,
And lots of water, yes, yes please!

We're going to the beach, hurray!
We're going to the sea!

Leaflets   Safety in the sun

Unit 8

Fish

Learn about freshwater and saltwater fish.

11 Look, listen and repeat. 2.47

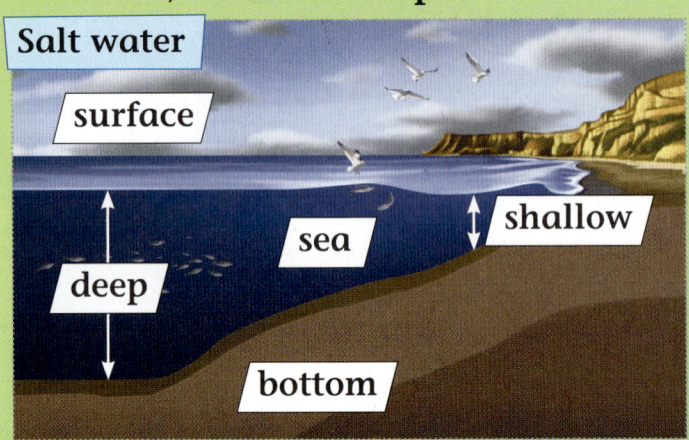

Salt water: surface, sea, shallow, deep, bottom

Fresh water: lake, river

12 Do the quiz. *True* or *false*?

QUIZ
1. All fish live near the surface of the water.
2. Some fish never see daylight.
3. Saltwater fish always live in the sea.
4. Some fish can live in salt water and fresh water.

13 Listen, read and check your answers. 2.48

Fish live in water. Fish live in seas, rivers and lakes.

Different fish live in very different places. Small fish need hiding places to escape from bigger fish.

Some fish live near the surface. Some fish live on the bottom. Some fish live at the bottom of the deepest oceans and never see daylight! These fish have big mouths, like the anglerfish. Some fish make their own light, like the lanternfish.

The quantity of salt in the water is very important. Most lakes and rivers are fresh water. Fresh water has much less salt than the ocean. Most freshwater fish cannot live in salt water. Pike and trout are freshwater fish.

Most saltwater fish cannot live in fresh water. Cod and sardines are saltwater fish. They live in the sea.

Some fish can live in both fresh and salt water. Salmon live in salt water, but swim up rivers to lay their eggs. Eels live in fresh water but swim to the sea to lay their eggs.

Aquatic life

14 Listen and find. 🔊 2.49

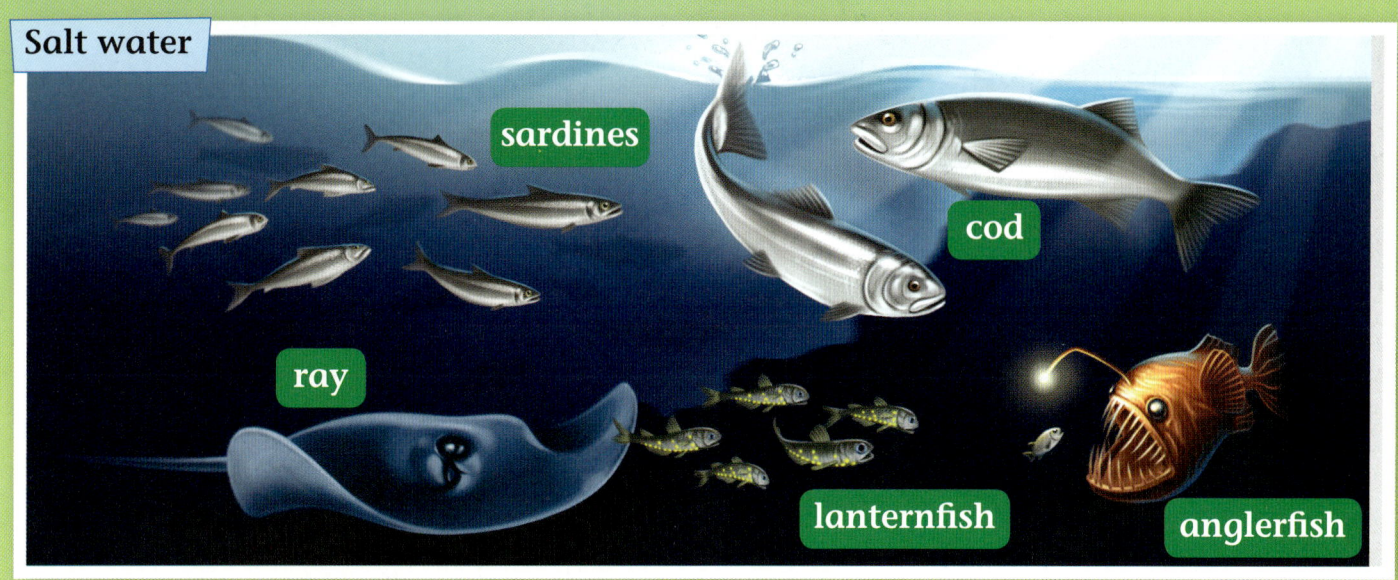

Salt water

sardines
cod
ray
lanternfish
anglerfish

Fresh water

trout
pike

15 Ask and answer.

Which fish do you like?

I like the ray. It lives in salt water. It lives near the bottom.

Talk about it!

I like **the ray**.   sardine cod trout
              anglerfish pike lanternfish

It lives in **salt water**.   fresh water

It lives **near the bottom**.   near the surface
                  in the deepest oceans

Science

Unit 8 · 65

16 Make fish tanks. PMB page 43

1 Draw.   **2** Colour.   **3** Write.

17 Listen, find and repeat. 2.50   **18** Listen and say the chant. 2.51

chant

aʊ — mouse
eɪ — snake
eə — stairs

Did you go to the old dark house?
Yes, we did, we saw a mouse.
We saw a spider, we saw a snake.
It was very big, it made me shake!

Were you frightened, were you scared?
Yes, we were, we ran downstairs.

66 Unit 8   Science   Pronunciation [aʊ] [eɪ] [eə]

9 Technology

1 Look, listen and repeat. 3.1   **2** Listen and find. 3.2

| 1 TV | 2 radio | 3 text message | 4 laptop | 5 mouse | 6 screen |
| 7 keyboard | 8 computer | 9 memory stick | 10 camera | 11 mobile phone |

3 Ask and answer.

- Does she need a mouse? — Yes, she does.
- Does she need a radio? — No, she doesn't.

Electrical items

Unit 9 67

4 We saved the club!

1. So tell us – what happened yesterday?

2. Well, we had a great day. There was a football match. MISSED!

3. Then there were some fireworks, but Coco was scared and went into the club.

4. But a burglar opened the window and climbed in. He wanted the new computer. Did you see the burglar?

5. No, the fireworks were very loud – we didn't see or hear anything.

6. The burglar tried to take the computer. But then he fell over Coco … CRASH!

He wanted the new computer. We didn't hear anything

7 We all chased the burglar. He ran very fast, but we ran fast too!

8 GOAL!
And then he fell over the balls!
And he fell into the goal!

9 And then we got him!

10 Well done! You saved the Incredible Club! You really are incredible!
Hurray!

DAILY NEWS
INCREDIBLE KIDS SAVE THEIR CLUB

5 Read and match.

1 The children played
2 Archie didn't get
3 Coco didn't like
4 The burglar came in through
5 The burglar wanted
6 The burglar fell over
7 The children saved
8 A photo of the children is in

a the Incredible Club.
b the window.
c football.
d the newspaper.
e the fireworks.
f Coco.
g a goal.
h the new computer

Unit 9 **69**

6 Which sentence is in the story? Make more sentences. PMB page 46

| He | wanted | the new computer | . |

| I | didn't want | the camera | . |

She

opened   We

the phone

the window   didn't open   the radio   the door

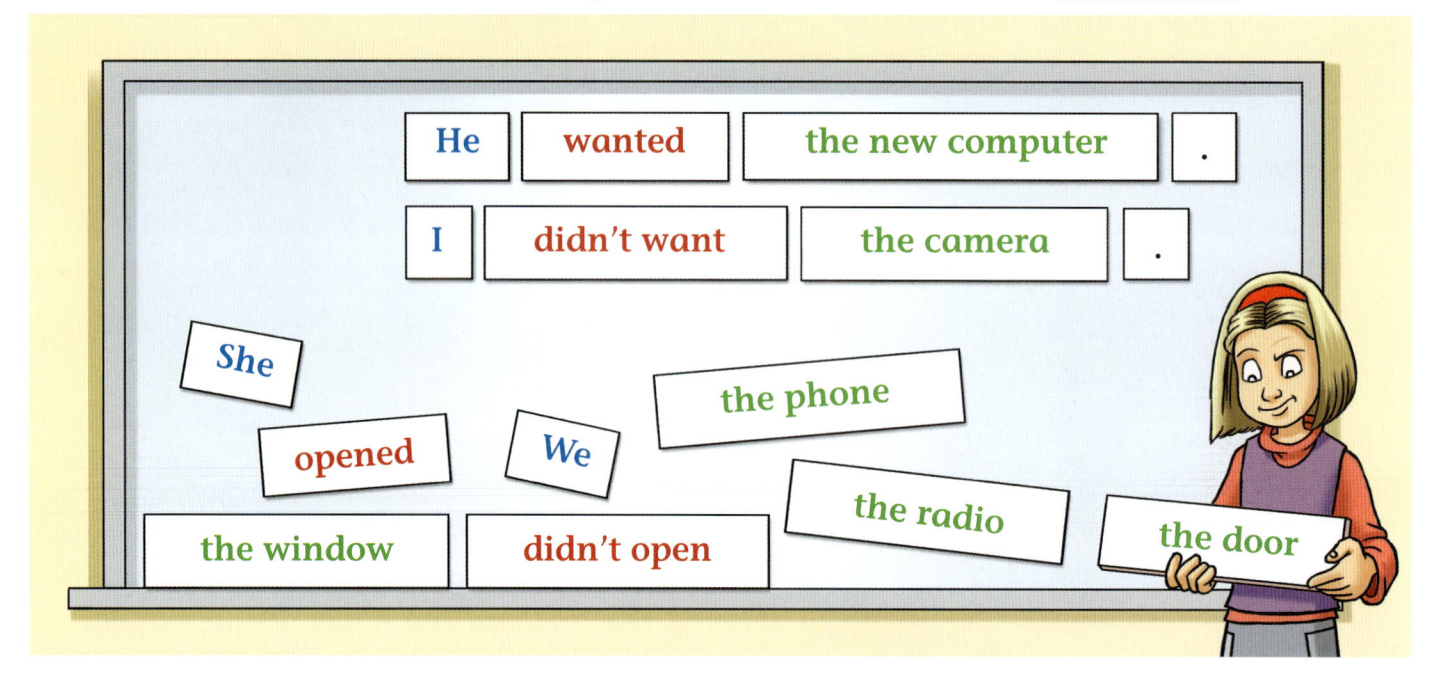

7 Listen and say which picture. 3.5

1 2 3 4

5 6 7 8

8 Ask and answer.

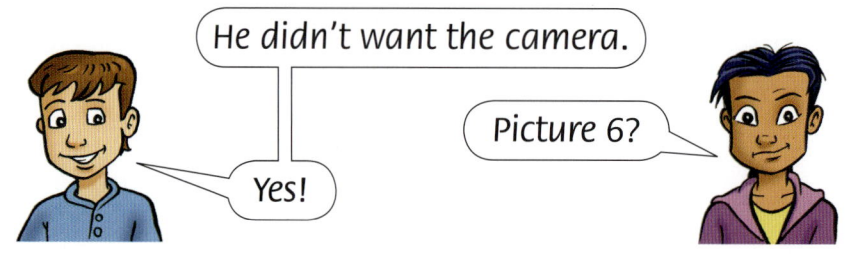

He didn't want the camera.

Yes!

Picture 6?

He wanted the computer. He didn't want the phone.

9 Read and say which game.

Instructions

A Stop thief!

You've got a new mobile phone. But thieves want to steal it! You want to arrive safely at home, but the thieves are running after you. Run as fast as you can! If a thief catches you, you lose a life. If you find a policeman, you get a new life.

B BANANAS FOR THE MONKEY

You are the monkey. You must go to the other side of the river to get the bananas. Jump across the stones but be careful! The crocodiles want to eat you. You mustn't jump on the crocodiles or fall in the river.

C Wave Rider

You are the boy on the surfboard. You want to arrive safely on the beach. You must catch beachballs to get bonus points. Touch people swimming in the sea for more energy. If you touch a shark or an octopus you lose a life.

1 You want the balls.
2 You want the fruit.
3 You want to arrive safely at home.
4 You mustn't fall in the water.
5 You must run very fast.
6 You want to arrive safely on the beach.

10 Listen and read. Then sing the song. 3.8

song

Keep in touch by letter,
Keep in touch by card,
Keep in touch by visiting,
It's really not that hard.

Keep in touch by email,
Keep in touch by phone,
Keep in touch by texting,
You're never far from home!

Instructions   Keeping in touch   Unit 9 **71**

Sending messages

Learn about different types of messages.

11 Look, listen and repeat. 3.9

Messages you can see

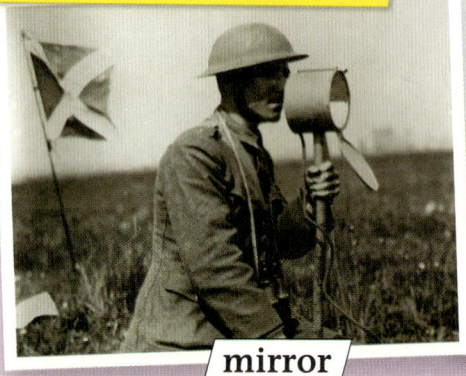

mirror

smoke

flags

Messages you can hear

Morse code

drums

Messages using animals

horse

pigeon

12 Answer the questions.

1 How do you communicate?
 a by phone   b by text message   c by email   d by letter   e all of these
2 What's your favourite way of sending a message?

Unit 9

Types of messages

13 Listen, read and answer. 🔊 3.10   **14** Then listen and find. 🔊 3.11

People always want to communicate ideas and information. For hundreds of years, people wrote letters. Today it's very easy to phone your friends or email them. But we can communicate in many other ways too.

Sometimes we send messages we can hear. Can you find two pictures where we can hear the message?

With Morse code, you use long and short sounds for letters of the alphabet. You listen to the sounds and write the letters. People used Morse code in early radio communication.

Sometimes we send messages we can see. We can use mirrors. Can you find the picture? People still use mirrors for mountain emergencies. If you are lost, you can signal to rescue planes.

We can also light a fire and use the smoke. People used smoke to send simple messages over long distances. Can you find the picture?

Sometimes we use animals to help us send our message. The Pony Express was a famous postal service in the USA. Which two animals can you see? Which animal did they use in the Pony Express?

We can also use flags. Semaphore is a system for sending messages with flags. People on ships often used it. You have two flags – one in each hand. You can make different letters and spell words. Can you find the picture?

Talk about it!

Can you **hear** this message?
see
Is it sending a message with **flags**?
Morse code?
smoke?
mirrors?
drums?

15 Ask and answer.

Can you hear this message? — Yes, you can.

Is it sending a message with drums? — Yes, it is.

History   Unit 9   73

16 Make a message. PMB page 48

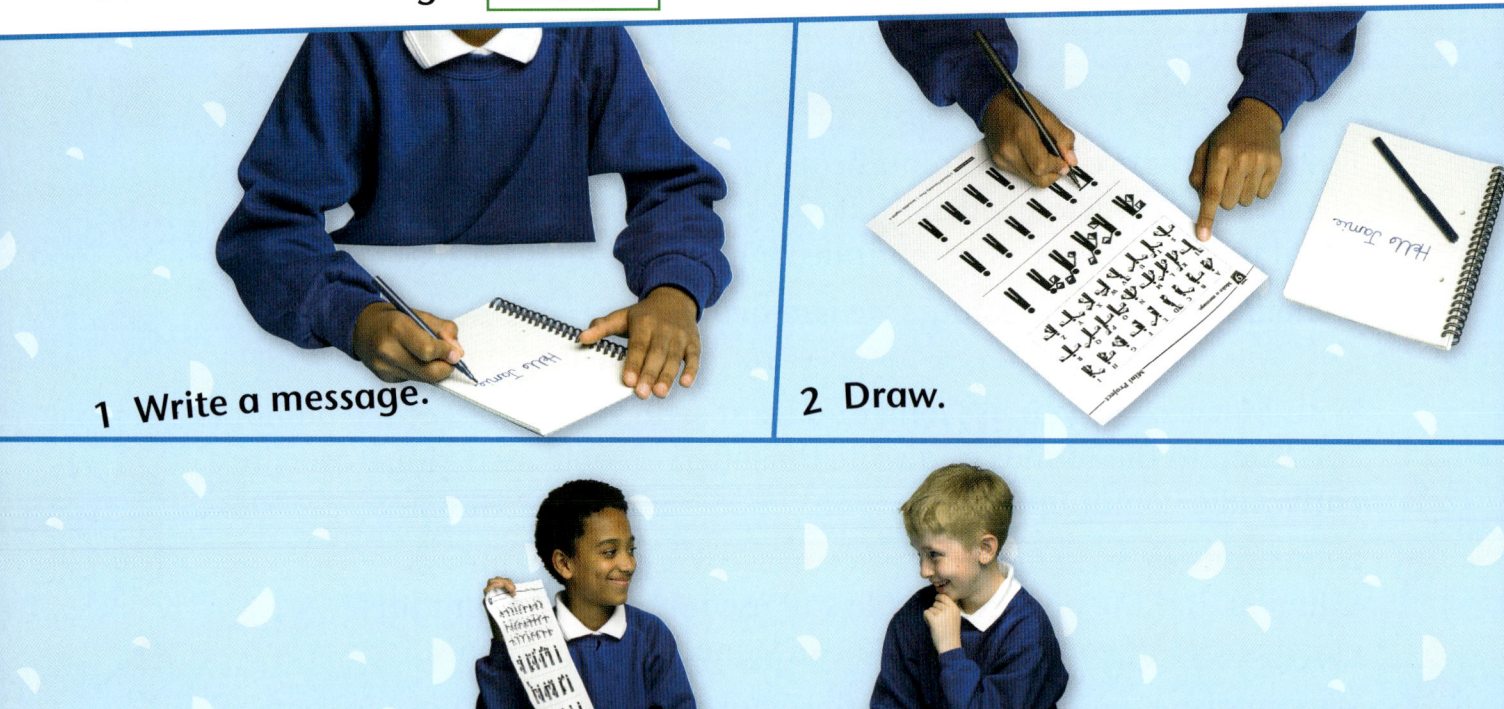

1 Write a message.

2 Draw.

3 Play.

17 Listen, find and repeat. 3.12   **18** Listen and say the chant. 3.13

chant

| t | d | ɪd |

danced   played   wanted

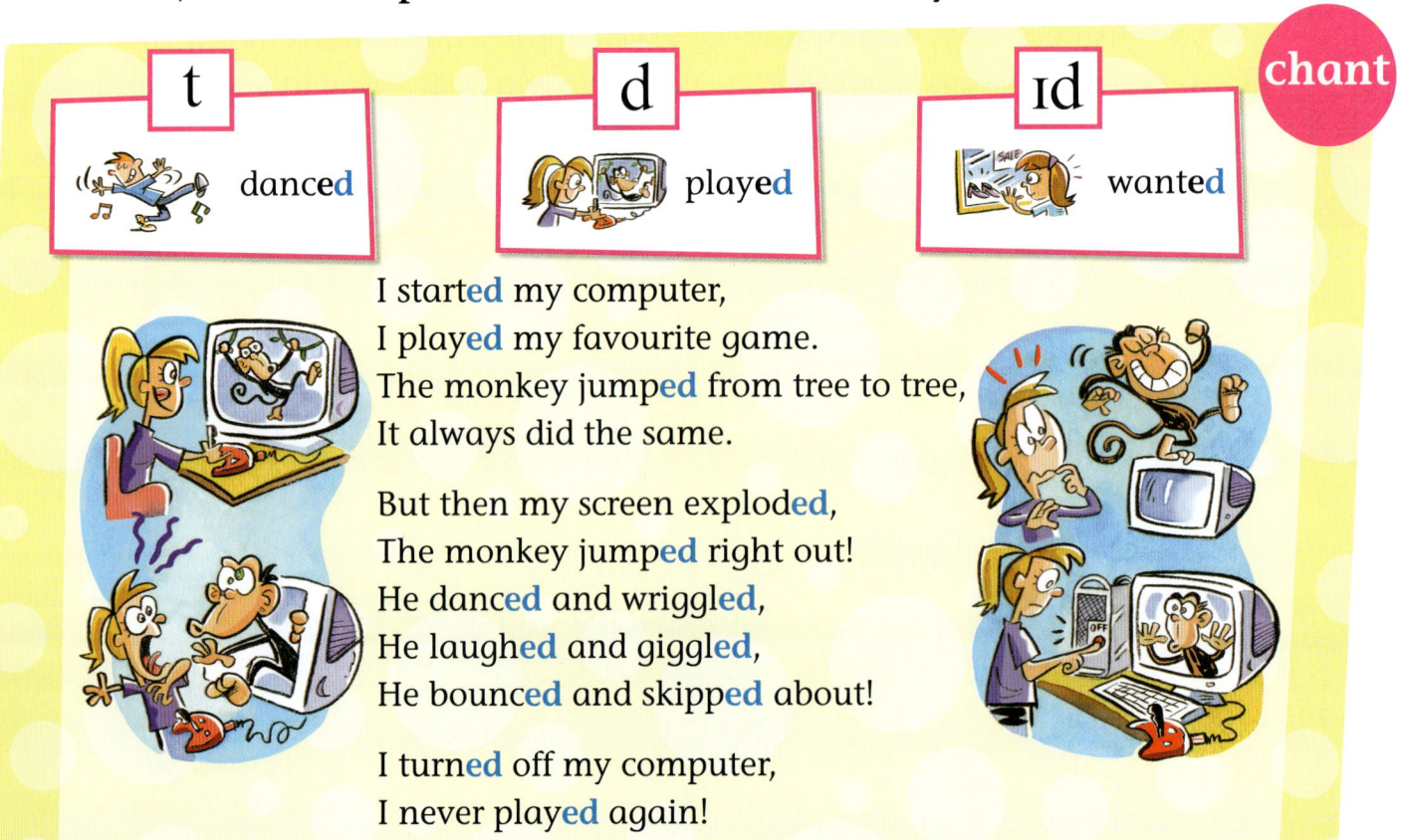

I started my computer,
I played my favourite game.
The monkey jumped from tree to tree,
It always did the same.

But then my screen exploded,
The monkey jumped right out!
He danced and wriggled,
He laughed and giggled,
He bounced and skipped about!

I turned off my computer,
I never played again!

History   Pronunciation [t] [d] [ɪd]

Advent

1 Listen and repeat. 🔊 3.14   **2** Read and find. Say.

| angel | candy cane | snowman | star | sleigh |
| Christmas tree | present | reindeer | Christmas pudding | stocking |

1 Father Christmas has one of these. He rides in it. A team of reindeer pull it.

2 It's green. At Christmas we put lots of pretty decorations on it.

3 It's got eyes and ears and a nose. Sometimes it has a hat and a scarf. It's very cold!

4 We eat this after Christmas dinner.

5 It's got coloured paper, ribbon and a label. We give these to friends and family at Christmas.

6 Father Christmas puts small presents in this. It looks like a big sock!

3 Listen and say the number. 🔊 3.15

4 Listen and sing the song. 🔊 3.16

Advent 75

Pancake Day

1 Listen and repeat. 3.17   **2** Look and find.

nuts   chocolate sauce   syrup   sugar   lemon   honey   jam   strawberries

3 Listen and find. 3.18

4 Read and match.

Do you like my pancake? It's got chocolate sauce and nuts.

My pancake is lovely. I don't like lots of sweet things so it's only got lemon, strawberries, and a little sugar.

Mmm! I like syrup. My pancake's got syrup and nuts. It hasn't got any chocolate.

I like all of the toppings. But on my pancake I've got my favourite – jam.

World Book Day

1 Look, listen and repeat. 3.19   **2** Listen and find. 3.20

adventure   comic   story   heroes   superheroes   mystery   fairy tale

3 Read and match.

a. I like fairy tales and adventures. I don't like mystery books.

b. I like comics about superheroes and I also like adventures. I don't like fairy tales at all!

c. I love story books about girls and I like mystery books. I never read comics.

d. I like true stories about sports heroes. I don't like mystery books.

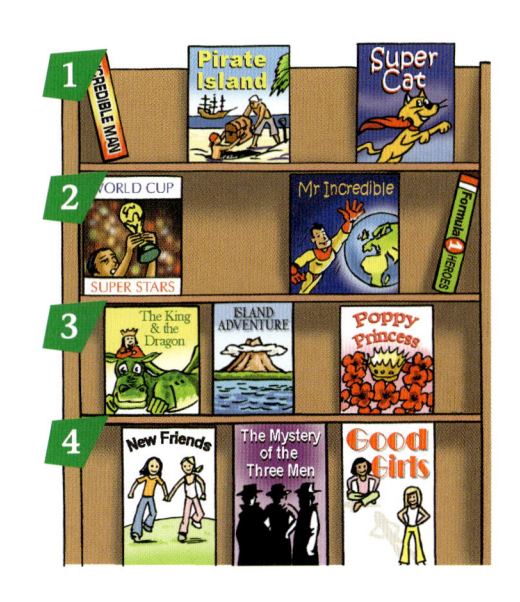

4 Ask and answer.

What's your favourite book? It's called Incredible Man.

What's it about? It's about a superhero. He is very strong and he helps people.

Children around the world — My country

1 Read and find the country.

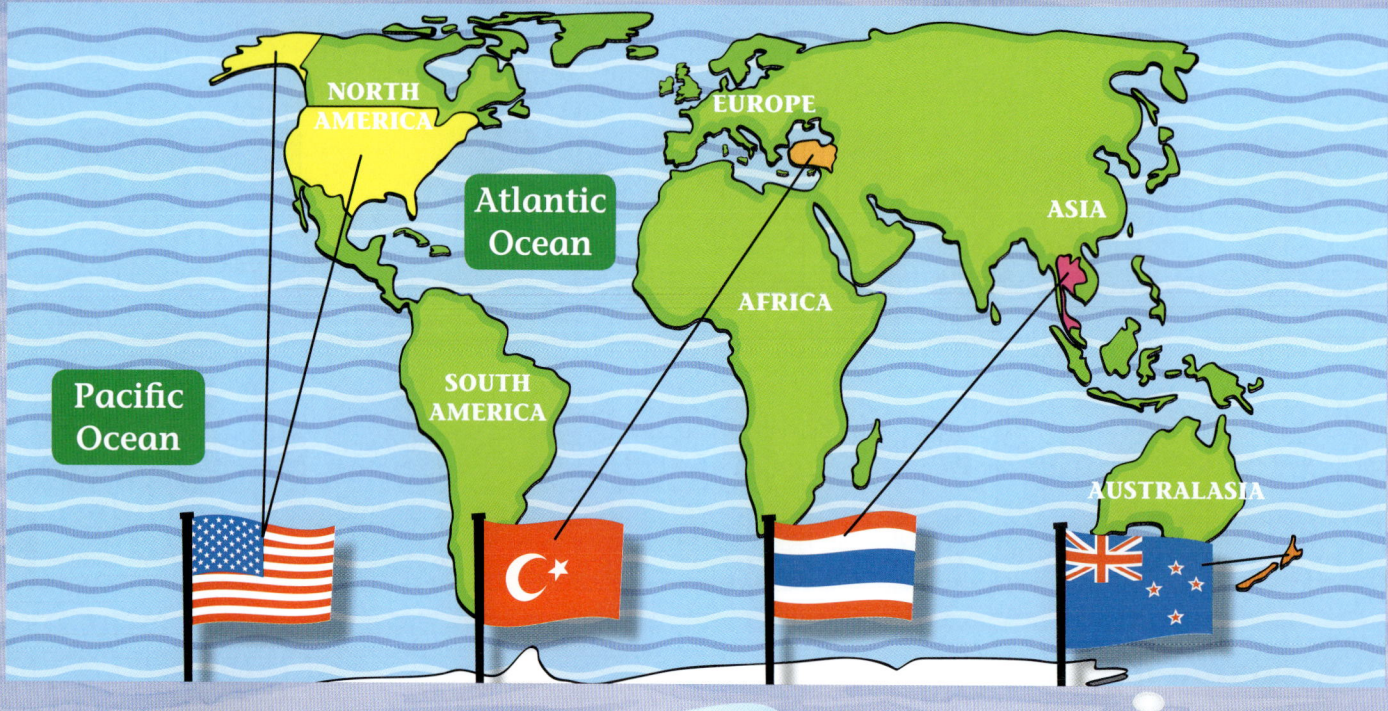

My name's Jacob. I'm from the United States of America and I live in Alaska. Alaska is in North America. There are lots of mountains here.

My name's Kemal. I'm from Turkey. Turkey is a big country, and there are beaches here. There are also forests, lakes, rivers and mountains.

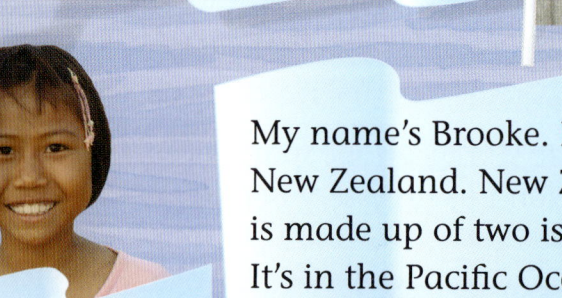

My name's Brooke. I'm from New Zealand. New Zealand is made up of two islands. It's in the Pacific Ocean. It's got volcanoes!

My name's Sunee. I live in a big city in Thailand. Thailand is in Asia. It's got mountains in the north and lots of beaches in the south.

2 Listen and match. 3.21

a

Look at the snow. It's freezing!

b

It's chilly here in winter.

c

Look at the rain. That's a monsoon!

d

What a warm and sunny day.

3 Read and say *true* or *false*.

1 You can go sailing in New Zealand.
2 It snows in Kemal's city sometimes.
3 You can climb mountains in Thailand.
4 Jacob lives in America.
5 Turkey is in Africa.
6 Sunee lives in a very dry country.
7 You can ski in Alaska.
8 Brooke lives near the Atlantic ocean.

Children around the world

Children around the world
My journey to school

1 Read. Then listen and match. 🔊 3.23

Sunee   Jacob   Brooke   Kemal

tuk tuk

school bus

snowmobile

tram

on foot

ferry

2 Ask and answer.

How does Brooke go to school?

She goes to school by school bus.

80 Children around the world

3 Look at the pictures. Whose journey is it?

4 Read and match the pictures to the sentences.
Then look at the pictures again and describe the journey.

Then he takes the ferry across the water.
First, Kemal buys a snack for his journey at the ferry port.
Finally, he takes the tram to school.

She buys a snack there for her journey.
Then she finds a tuk tuk and rides to school.
Sunee walks past the market on her way to school.

Children around the world **81**

Children around the world

My school

1 Listen and match. 🔊 3.25

Brooke   Kemal   Sunee   Jacob

Information Technology

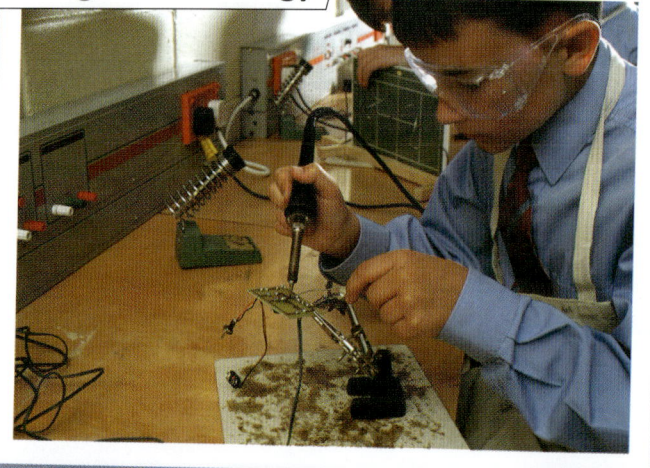

Drama

Design Technology

Art and Design

2 Ask and answer.

What's Kemal's favourite subject?

His favourite subject's Information Technology.

3 Look, read and say Brooke or Jacob.

School in New Zealand

School in Alaska

1 My school is very small, but it's got a lovely garden to play in.
2 My school is big. Many children travel from far away to come here.
3 We usually have the windows open in our classroom.
4 We have break time indoors because it's too cold outside.
5 We don't wear uniforms, but we wear big coats.
6 Our summer uniform has got shorts – even our teacher wears shorts!

Children around the world

Syllabus

Unit	Structures	Vocabulary	'Learning through English' topic and language
1	**Collocations with *go/play*** go climbing / rollerblading / fishing / rowing / sailing / skateboarding / swimming / water skiing play tennis / football / basketball / hide and seek / **Present Simple (*want to* + verb)** I want to (play basketball). I don't want to (go swimming). ***Let's* + verb** Let's (go sailing). ***can* (for ability)** Can you (swim)? Yes, I can. / No, I can't. ***You can…* (for possibility)** You can (go swimming) on Monday.	**Outdoor activities** climb, fish, play basketball, play football, play hide and seek, play tennis, rollerblade, row, sail, skateboard, swim, waterski	Geography: The water cycle and the weather **Weather** sunny, cloudy, windy, raining, snowing, foggy, stormy, (10) degrees, minus (5)
2	**Present Simple (for daily routine)** She gets up (at six o'clock). I go to bed (at eight o'clock). **Prepositions** Where's (Finn)? He's behind (the doctor). behind / next to / in front of / under / on **Adverbs of frequency with present simple** She always (gets up at seven o'clock). always / usually / never	**Jobs** actor, artist, astronaut, dancer, doctor, firefighter, footballer, pilot, pirate, policeman, scientist, teacher	Art: Drawing with a grid **Buildings** clock, lift, restaurant, stairs, tower
3	***should*** You should (sit down). You shouldn't (eat sweets). **Object pronouns** Can (you) help me? I can help (you). us / them / him / her / you / me ***I've got* (+illnesses)** What's the matter? I've got (a headache).	**Health** I feel … dizzy / sick. I've got … a cold / a cough / an earache / a headache / a sore throat / a stomach ache / a toothache.	Science: Pulse rates **Hand and heart** blood, fingers, heart, thumb, wrist, pulse
4	***some/any*** There's some (water). There isn't any (cheese). There are some (tomatoes). There aren't any (beans). **Present continuous** What's (she) doing? (She's watering the tomatoes).	**Farming** beans, cauliflower, goat, grass, milk, onions, peppers, potatoes, strawberries, tomatoes, water, weeds	Science: How plants grow **Habitats** hot, sunny, dry, wet, cold, shady

Unit	Structures	Vocabulary	'Learning through English' topic and language
5	**Comparatives** (Billy's) faster than (Coco). (Coco's) thinner than (Billy). **Superlatives** (Billy's) the biggest. (Coco's) the best. **Is it …?** Is it (slow)? Yes it is. / No it isn't.	**Adjectives of appearance** big, fast, fat, hungry, long, short, slow, small, strong, tall, thin	*Science: Bees* **Bees** beehive, comb, honey, queen, (worker), (drone)
6	**must / mustn't** You must (wear a helmet). You musn't (cross the road). **Can (for permission)** Can I (go and play)? Can I (have a biscuit)? **Directions** Go left/right at (the stop sign). Stop at the (traffic lights).	**Road safety** bike, car, gloves, go left, go right, helmet, road, sign, stop, traffic lights, zebra crossing	*Maths: Speed* **Numbers 100 – 1000** 100, 200, 300, 400, 500, 600, 700, 800, 900, 1000
7	**Past simple (*was / wasn't*)** I was (good at History). I wasn't (good at Maths). **Past simple questions and short answers (*was / wasn't*)** Were you (good at History)? Was he (good at Science)? Yes, I was. / No, he wasn't. **Present simple questions and short answers** Do you like (English)? Yes, I do. / No, I don't.	**School** Art, English, Geography, History, Maths, Music, P.E., Science, Spanish, classroom, poster	*History: Ancient Egypt* **Ancient Egypt** god, goddess, headdress, mummy, pharaoh, pyramid
8	**Past simple (irregular verbs)** I saw (an octopus). I didn't see (a shark). **Past simple questions and short answers** Did you go (to the beach)? Yes, I did. No I didn't. **Questions about quantity** How many (fish are there)? There are lots of (fish).	**Sea life** boat, crab, dolphin, fish, jellyfish, octopus, sand, seahorse, shark, shell, water, starfish	*Science: Fish* **Aquatic life** bottom, deep, lake, river, sea, shallow, surface
9	**Past simple (regular verbs)** He wanted (a computer). He didn't want (a phone). Did he (play on the computer?) Yes he did. / No, he didn't. **Present simple** Does she need a mouse? Yes, she does. / No, she doesn't.	**Electrical items** camera, computer, keyboard, laptop, memory stick, mobile phone, mouse, radio, screen, text message, TV	*History: Sending messages* **Messages** flags, horse, mirror, Morse code, pigeon, smoke, drums

Wordlist

Unit 1
Can I try it? /kən aɪ ˈtraɪ ɪt/
climb /klaɪm/
cloudy /ˈklaʊdi/
condensation /ˌkɒndenˈseɪʃn/
countryside /ˈkʌntrisaɪd/
degrees /dɪˈgriːz/
evaporation /ɪˌvæpəˈreɪʃn/
fish /fɪʃ/
foggy /ˈfɒgi/
Great idea! /ˈgreɪt aɪdɪə/
Here we go! /ˈhɪə wi: gəʊ/
I don't feel like…
 /aɪ dəʊnt ˈfiːl laɪk …/
Let's go … /lets ˈgəʊ …/
minus /ˈmaɪnəs/
play basketball
 /pleɪ ˈbɑːskɪtbɔːl/
play football /pleɪ ˈfʊtbɔːl/
play hide and seek
 /pleɪ haɪd ən ˈsiːk/
play tennis /pleɪ ˈtenɪs/
rain drops /ˈreɪn drɒps/
raining /ˈreɪnɪŋ/
rollerblade /ˈrəʊləbleɪd/
row /rəʊ/
sail /seɪl/
scooter /ˈskuːtə(r)/
Shh! /ʃ/
skateboard /ˈskeɪtbɔːd/
sky /skaɪ/
slide /slaɪd/
snowing /ˈsnəʊɪŋ/
standing /ˈstændɪŋ/
stormy /ˈstɔːmi/
sunny /ˈsʌni/
swim /swɪm/
swing /swɪŋ/
Wake up! /weɪk ˈʌp/
warm (v) /wɔːm/
water cycle /ˈwɔːtə saɪkl/
waterski /ˈwɔːtəskiː/
water vapour /ˈwɔːtə veɪpə/
weather /ˈweðə(r)/
What time is it?
 /wɒt ˈtaɪm ɪz ɪt/
What's the weather like?
 /wɒts ðə ˈweðə laɪk/
windy /ˈwɪndi/

Unit 2
actor / /
always /ˈɔːlweɪz/
artist /ˈɑːtɪst/
astronaut /ˈæstrənɔːt/
behind /bɪˈhaɪnd/
chief /tʃiːf/
clock /klɒk/
Come on! /ˈkʌm ɒn/
dancer /ˈdɑːnsə(r)/
doctor /ˈdɒktə(r)/
Don't worry! /dəʊnt ˈwʌri/
firefighter /ˈfaɪəfaɪtə(r)/
footballer /ˈfʊtbɔːlə(r)/
Good idea! /gʊd aɪˈdɪə/
grid /grɪd/
in front of /ɪn ˈfrʌnt əv/
It's … metres high.
 /ɪts … miːtəz ˈhaɪ/
It was built in …
 /ɪt wəz ˈbɪlt ɪn …/
lift (n) /lɪft/
never /ˈnevə/
next to /ˈnekst tu/
on /ɒn/
pilot /ˈpaɪlət/
pirate /ˈpaɪrət/
policeman /pəˈliːsmən/
restaurant /ˈrestrɒnt/
sailor /ˈseɪlə(r)/
scientist /ˈsaɪəntɪst/
singer /ˈsɪŋə(r)/
soldier /ˈsəʊldʒə(r)/
stairs /steəz/
teacher /ˈtiːtʃə(r)/
tower /ˈtaʊə(r)/
under /ˈʌndə/
usually /ˈjuːʒuəli/
What a mess! /wɒt ə ˈmes/

Unit 3
Are we nearly there?
 /ɑː wi nɪəli ˈðeə(r)/
beats per minute
 /biːts pə ˈmɪnɪt/
blood /blʌd/
bright /braɪt/
cheesecake /ˈtʃiːzkeɪk/
chicken /ˈtʃɪkɪn/
cold /kəʊld/
cough /kɒf/
dish /dɪʃ/
dizzy /ˈdɪzi/
earache /ˈɪəreɪk/
fingers /ˈfɪŋgəz/
fit /fɪt/
headache /ˈhedeɪk/
heart /hɑːt/
Hurrah! /həˈrɑː/
I can't wait! /aɪ kɑːnt ˈweɪt/
I don't feel well.
 /aɪ dəʊnt fiːl ˈwel/
I feel … /aɪ fiːl …/
I've got … /aɪv gɒt …/
measure /ˈmeʒə(r)/
Oh dear. /əʊ ˈdɪə(r)/
press (v) /pres/
pulse /pʌls/
pump (v) /pʌmp/
shoes /ʃuːz/
sick /sɪk/
sore throat /sɔː ˈθrəʊt/
stomach ache /ˈstʌməkeɪk/
Take your pulse.
 /teɪk jɔː ˈpʌls/
thumb /θʌm/
toothache /ˈtuːθeɪk/
What's the matter?
 /wɒts ðə ˈmætə(r)/
wrist /rɪst/

Unit 4
beans /biːnz/
bucket /ˈbʌkɪt/
cactus, cacti
 /ˈkæktəs, ˈkæktaɪ/
cauliflower /ˈkɒlɪflaʊə(r)/
cold /kəʊld/
Don't forget to…
 /dəʊnt fəˈget tə …/
dry /draɪ/
escape /ɪsˈkeɪp/
fern /fɜːn/
gate /geɪt/
goat /gəʊt/
Good work, kids!
 /gʊd ˈwɜːk, kɪdz/
grass /grɑːs/
grow /grəʊ/
habitat /ˈhæbɪtæt/
hot /hɒt/
leaf, leaves /liːf, liːvz/
milk /mɪlk/
needle /ˈniːdl/
onions /ˈʌnjənz/
Ouch, that hurts!
 /aʊtʃ, ðæt ˈhɜːts/
palm tree /ˈpɑːm triː/
peppers /ˈpepəz/
photosynthesis
 /ˌfəʊtəʊˈsɪnθəsɪs/
pick /pɪk/
pine tree /ˈpaɪn triː/
plant (v) /plɑːnt/
potatoes /pəˈteɪtəʊz/
seed /siːd/
shady /ˈʃeɪdi/
spike /spaɪk/
strawberries /ˈstrɔːbəriz/
sunflower /ˈsʌnflaʊə(r)/
sunny /ˈsʌni/
tap (n) /tæp/
tomatoes /təˈmɑːtəʊz/
water (v) /ˈwɔːtə(r)/
Watch out! /wɒtʃ ˈaʊt/
weeds /wiːdz/
wet /wet/

Unit 5
beehive /ˈbiːhaɪv/
big /bɪg/
chop down /tʃɒp ˈdaʊn/
collect /kəˈlekt/
colony /ˈkɒləni/
comb /kəʊm/
crisps /krɪsps/
drone /drəʊn/
fast /fɑːst/
fat /fæt/
female /ˈfiːmeɪl/
Go on! /gəʊ ˈɒn/
honey /ˈhʌni/
hungry /ˈhʌŋgri/
lay eggs /leɪ ˈegz/
long /lɒŋ/
male /meɪl/
queen /kwiːn/
Save the animals!
 /ˈseɪv ði ˈænɪməlz/
short /ʃɔːt/
slow /sləʊ/
small /smɔːl/
social insect
 /ˈsəʊʃl ɪnsekt/
strong /strɒŋ/
tall /tɔːl/
thin /θɪn/
waste /weɪst/
worker /ˈwɜːkə(r)/
You're the best! /jɔː ðə ˈbest/
You can do it! /ˈjuː kən du ɪt/

Unit 6

120 one hundred and twenty /ˈwʌn hʌndrəd ən ˈtwenti/
360 three hundred and sixty /ˈθriː hʌndrəd ən ˈsɪksti/
1,228 one thousand, two hundred and twenty-eight /ˈwʌn θaʊznd tuː hʌndrəd ən twenti ˈeɪt/
26,000 twenty-six thousand /twenti sɪks ˈθaʊznd/
Be careful! /bi ˈkeəfl/
bike /baɪk/
car /kɑː(r)/
circus /ˈsɜːkəs/
city /ˈsɪti/
clown /klaʊn/
crazy /ˈkreɪzi/
Cross at the… /ˈkrɒs ət ðə …/
crown /kraʊn/
cycling /ˈsaɪklɪŋ/
distance /ˈdɪstəns/
gloves /ɡlʌvz/
Go left at the… /ɡəʊ ˈleft ət ðə …/
Go right at the… /ɡəʊ ˈraɪt ət ðə …/
helmet /ˈhelmɪt/
Hold on tight. /həʊld ɒn ˈtaɪt/
How far…? /haʊ ˈfɑː …/
How fast…? /haʊ ˈfɑːst …/
How long…? /haʊ ˈlɒŋ …/
(100) a hundred /ə ˈhʌndrəd/
kilometres per hour /ˈkɪləmiːtə pə(r) ˈaʊə(r)/
left /left/
Let's go! /lets ˈɡəʊ/
Look out! /lʊk ˈaʊt/
right /raɪt/
road /rəʊd/
rule /ruːl/
Safety first! /ˈseɪfti ˈfɜːst/
sign /saɪn/
speed /spiːd/
speed limit /spiːd ˈlɪmɪt/
stop /stɒp/
Stop at the… /ˈstɒp ət ðə …/
(1000) a thousand /ə ˈθaʊznd/
track /træk/
traffic lights /ˈtræfɪk laɪts/
travel /ˈtrævl/
Use your head! /juːz jə ˈhed/
Watch out! /wɒtʃ ˈaʊt/
zebra crossing /zebrə ˈkrɒsɪŋ/

Unit 7

Art /ɑːt/
ancient /ˈeɪnʃnt/
bandages /ˈbændɪdʒɪz/
believe /bɪˈliːv/
break /breɪk/
calculator /ˈkælkjəleɪtə(r)/
classroom /ˈklɑːsruːm/
dead /ded/
die /daɪ/
English /ˈɪŋɡlɪʃ/
feathers /ˈfeðəz/
Geography /ˈdʒɒɡrəfi/
god /ɡɒd/
goddess /ˈɡɒdes/
headdress /ˈheddres/
History /ˈhɪstri/
horns /hɔːnz/
lucky /ˈlʌki/
Maths /mæθs/
medal /ˈmedl/
mummy /ˈmʌmi/
Music /ˈmjuːzɪk/
No matter what. /nəʊ mætə ˈwɒt/
P.E. /piː ˈiː/
pharaoh /ˈfeərəʊ/
poster /ˈpəʊstə(r)/
pyramid /ˈpɪrəmɪd/
school lunches /skuːl ˈlʌntʃɪz/
Science /ˈsaɪəns/
Spanish /ˈspænɪʃ/
strict /strɪkt/
subject /ˈsʌbdʒɪkt/
terrible /ˈterəbl/
tomb /tuːm/

Unit 8

anglerfish /ˈæŋɡləfɪʃ/
beach /biːtʃ/
boat /bəʊt/
bottom /ˈbɒtm/
cod /kɒd/
crab /kræb/
daylight /ˈdeɪlaɪt/
deep /diːp/
dolphin /ˈdɒlfɪn/
fish /fɪʃ/
fish tank /fɪʃ tæŋk/
freshwater /ˈfreʃwɔːtə(r)/
frightened /ˈfraɪtnd/
jellyfish /ˈdʒelifɪʃ/
lake /leɪk/
lanternfish /ˈlæntənfɪʃ/
leaflet /ˈliːflət/
octopus /ˈɒktəpəs/
pike /paɪk/
ray /reɪ/
river /ˈrɪvə(r)/
saltwater /ˈsɒltwɔːtə(r)/
sand /sænd/
sardines /sɑːˈdiːnz/
sea /siː/
seahorse /ˈsiːhɔːs/
shake /ʃeɪk/
shallow /ˈʃæləʊ/
shark /ʃɑːk/
shell /ʃel/
She was a star! /ʃiː wəz ə ˈstɑː(r)/
show (n) /ʃəʊ/
starfish /ˈstɑːfɪʃ/
suncream /ˈsʌnkriːm/
surface /ˈsɜːfɪs/
trout /traʊt/
water (n) /ˈwɔːtə(r)/

Unit 9

bounce /baʊns/
burglar /ˈbɜːɡlə(r)/
camera /ˈkæmrə/
chase /tʃeɪs/
communicate /kəˈmjuːnɪkeɪt/
computer /kəmˈpjuːtə(r)/
drums /drʌmz/
explode /ɪkˈspləʊd/
fireworks /ˈfaɪəwɜːks/
flags /flæɡz/
giggle /ˈɡɪɡl/
horse /hɔːs/
Keep in touch. /kiːp ɪn ˈtʌtʃ/
keyboard /ˈkiːbɔːd/
laptop /ˈlæptɒp/
memory stick /ˈmemri stɪk/
message /ˈmesɪdʒ/
mirrors /ˈmɪrəz/
mobile phone /məʊbaɪl ˈfəʊn/
Morse code /mɔːs ˈkəʊd/
mouse /maʊs/
newspaper /ˈnjuːspeɪpə(r)/
pigeon /ˈpɪdʒɪn/
radio /ˈreɪdiəʊ/
screen /skriːn/
send /send/
smoke /sməʊk/
text message /ˈtekst mesɪdʒ/
thief, thieves /θiːf, θiːvz/
TV /tiː ˈviː/
What happened? /wɒt ˈhæpnd/
wriggle /ˈrɪɡl/

Festivals

advent /ˈædvent/
angel /ˈeɪndʒl/
candy cane /ˈkændi keɪn/
Christmas pudding /krɪsməs ˈpʊdɪŋ/
Christmas tree /ˈkrɪsməs triː/
present /ˈpreznt/
reindeer /ˈreɪndɪə(r)/
sleigh /sleɪ/
snowman /ˈsnəʊmæn/
star /stɑː(r)/
stocking /ˈstɒkɪŋ/

chocolate sauce /ˈtʃɒklət sɔːs/
honey /ˈhʌni/
jam /dʒæm/
lemon /ˈlemn/
nuts /nʌts/
pancake /ˈpænkeɪk/
strawberries /ˈstrɔːbəriz/
sugar /ˈʃʊɡə(r)/
syrup /ˈsɪrəp/

adventure /ədˈventʃə(r)/
comic /ˈkɒmɪk/
fairy tale /ˈfeəri teɪl/
heroes /ˈhɪərəʊz/
mystery /ˈmɪstəri/
story /ˈstɔːri/
superheroes /ˈsuːpəhɪərəʊz/

Children around the world

Alaska /əˈlæskə/
New Zealand /njuː ˈziːlənd/
Thailand /ˈtaɪlænd/
Turkey /ˈtɜːki/
United States of America /juːnaɪtɪd ˈsteɪts əv əˈmerɪkə/

chilly /ˈtʃɪli/
freezing /ˈfriːzɪŋ/
monsoon /mɒnˈsuːn/
volcano /vɒlˈkeɪnəʊ/
warm /wɔːm/

ferry /ˈferi/
journey /ˈdʒɜːni/
on foot /ɒn ˈfʊt/
school bus /skuːl bʌs/
snowmobile /ˈsnəʊməbiːl/
tram /træm/
tuk tuk /ˈtʌk tʌk/

Art and Design /ɑːt ən dɪˈzaɪn/
Design Technology /dɪˈzaɪn tekˈnɒlədʒi/
Drama /ˈdrɑːmə/
Information Technology /ɪnfəˈmeɪʃn tekˈnɒlədʒi/

OXFORD
UNIVERSITY PRESS

Great Clarendon Street, Oxford OX2 6DP

Oxford University Press is a department of the University of Oxford.
It furthers the University's objective of excellence in research, scholarship,
and education by publishing worldwide in

Oxford   New York

Auckland   Cape Town   Dar es Salaam   Hong Kong   Karachi
Kuala Lumpur   Madrid   Melbourne   Mexico City   Nairobi
New Delhi   Shanghai   Taipei   Toronto

With offices in

Argentina   Austria   Brazil   Chile   Czech Republic   France   Greece
Guatemala   Hungary   Italy   Japan   Poland   Portugal   Singapore
South Korea   Switzerland   Thailand   Turkey   Ukraine   Vietnam

OXFORD and OXFORD ENGLISH are registered trade marks of
Oxford University Press in the UK and in certain other countries

© Oxford University Press 2007
The moral rights of the author have been asserted
Database right Oxford University Press (maker)
First published 2007
2012   2011   2010
10   9   8   7

No unauthorized photocopying

All rights reserved. No part of this publication may be reproduced,
stored in a retrieval system, or transmitted, in any form or by any means,
without the prior permission in writing of Oxford University Press,
or as expressly permitted by law, or under terms agreed with the appropriate
reprographics rights organization. Enquiries concerning reproduction
outside the scope of the above should be sent to the ELT Rights Department,
Oxford University Press, at the address above

You must not circulate this book in any other binding or cover
and you must impose this same condition on any acquirer

Any websites referred to in this publication are in the public domain and
their addresses are provided by Oxford University Press for information only.
Oxford University Press disclaims any responsibility for the content

ISBN: 978 0 19 444010 3

Printed in China

ACKNOWLEDGEMENTS

The authors and publishers would like to thank the following teachers for their help in developing the course: Catherine Anner, Agnieszka Bajerlain, Sonia Bonjorn, Rosario Brondolo, Claire Carril Rama and all at Colegio Alca in Milladoiro, Beata Chmielewska, Joanna Cudowska-Kolendo, Karolina Gogolewska, Joanna Herok, Aine Kiely, Gladys Ledwith, Silvia Luppi, Magdalena Łapczuk, Julie Mills, Izabela Pastewska, Szymon Polakowski, Ewa Rowińska, Richard Savage.

The publishers advise that project work involving cutting and sticking should be carried out under the supervision of an adult.

Main illustrations by: Paul Gibbs pp 3, 6, 11, 14, 15, 19, 22, 23, 27, 30, 31, 35, 38, 43, 46, 47, 51, 54, 55, 59, 62, 67, 70, 71, 75, 76, 77.

Song artwork by: Garry Parsons pp 7, 15, 23, 31, 39, 47, 55, 63, 71.

Pronunciation chant illustrations by: Dave Whammond/3 in a Box pp 10, 18, 26, 34, 42, 50, 58, 66, 74.

Story illustrations by: Paul Gibbs and John Haslam pp 4, 5, 12, 13, 20, 21, 28, 29, 36, 37, 44, 45, 52, 53, 60, 61, 68, 69.

Other illustrations by: Adrian Barclay/Beehive Illustration pp 8, 9, 24, 32, 33, 41, 56; Kathy Baxendale pp 16, 17; Mark Ruffle pp 78, 80, 82; Myles Talbot pp 64, 65.

Cover illustration by: Paul Gibbs.

Commissioned photography: Gareth Boden pp 10, 18, 24, 25, 26, 34, 42, 50, 58, 66, 73, 74.

The Publishers would also like to thank the following for their kind permission to reproduce photographs and other copyright material: Alamy pp 33 (Cosmo Condina/sunflowers, James Osmond/pine trees, CuboImages srl/cacti, Art Kowalsky/palm trees, Chad Ehlers/ferns), 39 (David Fleetham/blue whale), 48 (WoodyStock/speedometer), 49 (Motoring Picture Library/car in town, SUNNYphotography.com/plane), 56 (Rolf Richardson/pyramid, Bygonetimes/pharaoh, CuboImages srl/mummy), 57 (Bygonetimes/Horus, Gary Cook/Sobek, Visual Arts Library/Bastet), 63 (Bill Bachman/water world, Brandon Cole Marine Photography/jellyfish/dolphins, Stephen Frink Collection/sharks), 64 (ACE STOCK LIMITED/small fish, David R. Frazier Photolibrary/trout), 78 (Rebecca Erol/Kemal, Cris Haigh/Sunee), 79 (Images&Stories/Istanbul and snow, Andrew Woodley/rain, Hideo Kurihara/New Zealand in sun), 80 (Jon Arnold Images/tuk-tuk, Brian & Cherry Alexander Photography/snow mobile, JTB Photo Communications, Inc./metro, Photofusion Picture Library/walk, Ray Roberts/ferry), 81 (Robert Harding Picture Library Ltd/ferry port, Vikki Martin/street vendor, Eddie Gerald/metro, Helmuth Rieger/food seller Chiang Mai, David Norton/market), 82 (Helene Rogers/computer class, Roger Bamber/drama, Photofusion Picture Library/pottery), 83 (Bryan & Cherry Alexander Photography/Alaska school exterior); Ardea pp 39 (Tom & Pat Leeson/African elephant), 40 (Steve Hopkin/queen bee); Corbis pp 56 (Sandro Vannini/god, Dallas & John Heaton/Free Agents Ltd/goddess), 57 (Gianni Dagli Orti/Osiris/Tefnut, Roger Wood/Isis), 72 (Bettmann/semaphore/pony express/Phillip Gendreau/pigeon, Hulton Deutsch Collection/mirror signal), 79 (Paul A. Sounders/Alska snow), 81 (Macduff Everton/tuk-tuk stand), 83 (James L. Amos/NZ school interior, Galen Rowell/Alaska school interior); Education Photos p82 (John Walmsley/DT class); FLPA p 40 (Michael Durham/Minden Pictures/worker bee); Getty Images pp 16 (Chris Tomaidis/Stone/CN Tower, Johner/Johner Images/Leaning Tower of Pisa, Gregor Schuster/Photonica), 17 (Stephen Alvarez/National Geographic/Eiffel Tower), 39 (Charles Sleicher/Stone/spider), 40 (Anita Oberhauser/Stockfood Creative/honey, Frank Greenaway/Dorling Kindersely/drone), 48 (Jamal Nasrallah/AFP/Getty Editorial/thrust), 49 (Jim Cummins/Taxi/walk, Andy Rouse/The Image Bank/cheetah, Vladimir Rys/Bongarts/Getty Editorial/racing car, Frank Whitney/The Image Bank/space shuttle), 72 (Meyer Pfundt/Hulton Archive/morse code), 78 (Frank Herholdt/Taxi/Jacob, Seth Joel/Taxi, Brooke); Lonely Planet Images pp 16 (Jonathan Smith/Palace of Science and Culture), 80 (Jon Davison/school bus), 83 (Denis O'Byrne/NZ school exterior); Mary Evans Picture Library p 72 (smoke signals/drum message); Nature Picture Library p 64 (David Shale/anglerfish); Papilio Photos p 40 (Robert Pickett/beehive).

Learning through English poster illustrations by: Adrian Barclay (posters 3, 4) Mark Ruffle (poster 6).

Learning through English posters: the Publishers would also like to thank the following for their kind permission to reproduce photographs and other copyright material:

Alamy Poster 1 (The Cholomondeley Sisters 1600-10/Tate Gallery/The Print Collector), Poster 2 (John Pickles/aphids, Rob Walls/stick insect, NaturePics/ants), Poster 3 (Ivan J Belcher/Worldwide Picture Library/Alice's shop, Alan Copson City Pictures/covered market, Pictor International/ImageState/punting, Michael Jenner/Robert Harding Picture Library Ltd/Sheldonian, David Stares/bus tour), Poster 4 (Mark Boulton/medium cloud, Kathy Wright/high cloud, Alaska Stock LCC/snow crystal), Poster 5 (Dallas and John Heaton/pyramids), Poster 6 (David Fleetham/crab, LHB Photo/eel, Jeff Rotman/mermaid's purse); Bridgeman Art Library Poster 1 (Two Sisters and a Brother of the Artist (oil on panel), Anguissola, Sofonisba (1527-1626)/Corsham Court, Wiltshire, Portrait of a Student, c.1918-19 (oil on canvas), Modigliani, Amedeo (1884-1920)/Solomon R. Guggenheim Museum, New York, USA, My Second Sermon (w/c), Millais, Sir John Everett (1829-96)/Victoria & Albert Museum, London, UK; The British Museum Poster 5 (© The Trustees of the British Museum/necklace, cat mummy, jewellery making, boat, fish, inspecting the fields, Book of the dead); Nature Picture Library Poster 6 (David Shale/octopus); Oxford Picture Library Poster 3 (Christ Church Dining Room); OUP RF Poster 2 (praying mantis, beetle, wings, butterfly, caterpillar, bees) Poster 4 (rainbow, low cloud, snow scene) Poster 6 (skate).

The Rollercoaster Game poster artwork by: Paul Gibbs.